ATTACK OF THE THEOCRATS

ATTACK OF THE THEOCRATS

How the Religious Right Harms Us All— and What We Can Do About It

Sean Faircloth

Foreword by Richard Dawkins

1909 STILLHOUSE ROAD

PITCHSTONE PUBLISHING
Charlottesville, Virginia 22901

PITCHSTONE PUBLISHING
Charlottesville, Virginia 22901

19 18 17 16 15 14 13 12   1 2 3 4 5

Library of Congress Cataloging-in-Publication Data

Faircloth, Sean.
  Attack of the theocrats! : how the religious right harms us all — and what we can do about it /
Sean Faircloth ; foreword by Richard Dawkins.
       p. cm.
  Includes bibliographical references and index.
  ISBN 978-0-9844932-4-1 (hardcover : alk. paper) — ISBN 978-0-9844932-5-8 (pbk. : alk. paper)
1. Church and state—United States. 2. United States—Church history. 3. Christianity and
politics—United States. I. Title.
  BR516.F25 2012
  322'.10973—dc23

                                                                    2011026904

This book is dedicated to my three sons, Brendan, Ryan, and Declan.
I am so proud of these funny, kind young men.

Contents

Foreword

The United States' Founding Fathers, giants of the eighteenth-century Enlightenment, were farseeing in their plans because they were wise in history. They knew the European past from which so many Americans had escaped, and they crafted a document of immunization against any such future. "Congress shall make no law respecting an establishment of religion, or prohibiting the free exercise thereof." In other words, while individuals are free to practice any religion they choose, *the United States shall never be a theocracy*.

That first clause of the Bill of Rights, precious First Amendment to the greatest constitutional document ever enacted, is—or ought to be—the envy of the world. My own country is still nominally a theocracy, with twenty-six unelected bishops sitting, ex officio, in Parliament; and with the head of state synonymous with head of the Church of England and constitutionally forbidden to be a Roman Catholic (let alone a Muslim or a Jew). To this day, the Catholic-Protestant divide poisons Northern Ireland and, in miniature, Glasgow on a soccer Saturday—indeed, during the rest of the week too, for Glaswegians well understand the coded meaning of "what school did you go to?" And Britain is still infested with state-subsidized "faith schools."

None of that would have surprised James Madison and his colleagues. It is exactly what they worked hard to forestall. But even they could not have foreseen the zealous nastiness of our twenty-first-century theocrats. In Saudi Arabia, for instance, Mustafa Ibrahim was judicially executed in 2007 for practicing "sorcery" (he was a pharmacist)—the same Saudi Arabia, our ally and oil provider, where a woman can be arrested for driving a car, for showing an arm or an ankle, or for being seen in public without a male relative (who may, as a generous concession, be a child). In Somalia, a thirteen-year-old girl, Aisho Ibrahim Dhuhulow, was sentenced in 2008 to death by

9

stoning, in front of a large crowd in a soccer stadium. Her crime of "adultery" was actually the crime—under sharia law—of being gang raped. After such horrors, the following, recorded of his country by a citizen of Israel in 2009, may serve as light relief by comparison:

> In no other country are there streets without buses and tracks without trains on the Sabbath. No other airline but El Al sits idle one day a week. Cold platters on the Sabbath in hospitals and hotels are also something not seen . . . and the separation in certain buses of men and women are also unknown in democratic countries. Religion has never been separate from the state here; hand in hand they oversee our way of life.

The United States is officially not a theocracy. Thomas Jefferson's wall of separation still stands—but precariously, enduring a ceaseless buffeting, a hammering, and insidious chipping away by (mainly Christian) saboteurs, who either ignorantly misread the Founders' intentions or willfully oppose them. And this is where Sean Faircloth rides in as a latter-day hero of the Constitution. His book is a timely—poignantly timely—manifesto of secularism (not atheism). His message is secularist and *conservative* in the true meaning of the term: conserving the original secularist principles of the Constitution—unlike the so-called conservatives of the Tea Party, whose aim, where religion is concerned, is unashamedly to undermine the core principle of the First Amendment. Sean Faircloth quotes Barry Goldwater: "I don't have any respect for the Religious Right." Though Faircloth was a liberal Democrat in the Maine State Senate, the following 1981 words of the arch conservative Senator Goldwater might have inspired this book.

> There is no position on which people are so immovable as their religious beliefs. There is no more powerful ally one can claim in a debate than Jesus Christ, or God, or Allah, or whatever one calls this supreme being. But like any powerful weapon, the use of God's name on one's behalf should be used sparingly. The religious factions that are growing throughout our land are not using their religious clout with wisdom. They are trying to force government leaders into following their position 100 percent. If you disagree with these religious groups on a particular moral issue, they complain, they threaten you with a loss of money or votes or both. I'm frankly sick and tired of the political preachers across this country telling me as a citizen that if I want to be a moral person, I must believe in

A, B, C, and D. Just who do they think they are? And from where do they presume to claim the right to dictate their moral beliefs to me? And I am even more angry as a legislator who must endure the threats of every religious group who thinks it has some God-granted right to control my vote on every roll call in the Senate. I am warning them today: I will fight them every step of the way if they try to dictate their moral convictions to all Americans in the name of conservatism.

Sean Faircloth was trained as a lawyer, and again and again his book uncovers the harm done to today's Americans by religious bias and privileging in law. The least fortunate suffer physical injury, torture, and even death. Putting a face on the faceless, giving a voice to the voiceless, Faircloth champions these innocent victims of religious privilege. They include two-year-old Amiyah White, who died unattended in the van of a Christian child-care center. Why mention that it was "Christian"? Because the tragedy followed directly from the center's religious exemption from state child-safety laws. In Tennessee in 2002, Jessica Crank died of cancer, aged fifteen, after her mother chose to have her malignancy treated by "faith healing" rather than scientific medicine. This useless "treatment" was administered under cover of a religious exemption from a state child-protection law.

Those are just two of many tragic stories. Countless other unfortunates who have suffered in the same way are lost footnotes to religion's privileged dodging of civilized law. Seeking to restore the human element, Sean Faircloth calls on his readers to share accounts of martyred children and other victims of ignorant piety. Personal stories serve as lamentable entry points into his charge sheet against America's theocratic politicians and hucksters. Readers may count the ways in which theocratic laws exact harm on American citizens—financially, socially, militarily, physically, emotionally, and educationally. But the "us all" to which his book's subtitle refers is not restricted to Americans. The "theocratic attack" that has been under way in the United States for more than three decades spills out into the world at large (which incidentally entitles me, as a non-American, to recommend this book).

Faircloth takes the death of fourteen-year-old Saron Samta from a botched back-alley abortion in Ethiopia, and links it to the global "gag rule," initiated under Ronald Reagan, which restricts women's access to basic health information and services. He recalls George W. Bush's infamous phone call to Jacques Chirac before the Iraq War, when Bush reportedly warned the French president that "Gog and Magog are at work in the

Middle East" and that "the biblical prophecies are being fulfilled." Such crass evangelical certitude, trotted out by a sitting U.S. president to another head of state, is chilling. One can only imagine what biblical chestnuts were served up and swallowed in the prayer sessions that Bush held with the equally devout Tony Blair while scheming for their war. The fundamentalists' undermining of American science has comparable international effects. The biblical idea of man's "dominion" has resonated through the environmental policies of Republican administrations and informs public views on climate change, thus contributing to the degradation of the whole planet.

As Faircloth reminds us, 535 members of Congress make laws for the other 300 million Americans. He names and shames the fifty most egregious theocrats among them (all but three of them Republicans), omitting those who merely vote for theocratic policies while not being vocal about them. He gives honorable mention to Congressman Pete Stark as the only one of the 535 who has publicly come out as a nonbeliever. He might have added that, in a country where 17 percent of the population are nonbelievers (25 percent of those under thirty), it is statistically vanishingly unlikely that Pete Stark is really the only nonbelieving American to have been elected to Congress. Given the additional fact that nonbelief is especially frequent among educated classes, the inference is inevitable that a substantial number of the other 534 would join Representative Stark if only they had his courage and his integrity. Perhaps they overestimate the votes to be gained by cynically sucking up to the pious.

Faircloth pays just attention to one of the great iniquities of the American taxation system, one shared with many other countries. Religious institutions, churches, even obscenely wealthy televangelists, are tax-exempt, and privileged to be free from much of the burden of even *declaring* money for taxation. As he writes:

- Unlike nonprofits, churches don't have to file 990 forms (a basic financial disclosure). Thus, their finances are the most secretive of any so-called charitable organization. For-profit businesses, of course, must file detailed tax documents. So must 501(c)(3) nonprofits. Because the finances of religious organizations are akin to the proverbial black box, it is difficult to even find out whether something improper has occurred.

- Only a "high-level" IRS official can even authorize an audit of a religious organization. Meanwhile, the rest of us—whether individuals, for-profit businesses, or secular nonprofits—can be audited by any old IRS bureaucrat.

- Religious groups can legally give tax-free housing allowances to so-called clergy (some of whom just might be family), allowances that are not counted as income, exempting the housing from taxation.

To return to my opening theme, Faircloth leaves us in no doubt that the Founding Fathers established a nation that should forever separate state from church. Every American child knows this, or at least used to know it (the Texas Board of Education's 2010 decision to question the separation of church and state in the state's social-studies curriculum awaits a more charitable interpretation than I can muster). By sage design, the United States was to be kept free of religion's suffocating foot so as to give breath to individual conscience. By putting into practice this cherished ideal, the United States civilized humankind. Other countries followed suit with their own secular constitutions, including, notably, France, Turkey, and India. If America, the world's standard-bearer of secular governance, allows fundamentalists, tipsy with faith, to erode the wall between church and state, whither the world?

Faircloth paints a sobering picture, but fortunately, as anyone who has heard his speeches knows, he also has an inspiring and invigorating vision to offer. His intention is not just to awaken people to how the Religious Right harms us all. He ends his book with a much-needed plan for action. As a shrewd former politician, and highly successful executive director of the Secular Coalition for America, Sean Faircloth is uniquely positioned to play a decisive role in returning America to its secular foundation. His concluding manifesto is the optimistic flipside to the dark picture that his earlier chapters present. Readers will finish the book exercised, energized, and eager to join Sean Faircloth in a bold rediscovery of the secular dream of the European Enlightenment and America's enlightened Fathers.

RICHARD DAWKINS
OXFORD, ENGLAND

Preface

Early in high school I had acne, braces, and perpetually crooked glasses. My parents dressed me in polyester and refused me the haircuts that were then fashionable. To understate matters, dating was a challenge. Oh, girls sometimes spoke to me. I recall one in particular saying, "Pizza face, railroad tracks, four-eyed geek!" Forever hunched over a book, I sought, and often found, an escape from, well, me. I needed to overcome my shyness, so my dad, a theater teacher, suggested I try out for a play at my high school.

Since elementary school, I had watched my father direct plays. Frequently, after my regular school day was done, I would tag along to the high school where my dad taught and watch rehearsals into the night. Dad's approach to directing students more closely resembled the stereotypical style of a football coach or baseball manager than that of an artistic director. Ethereal was not my dad's style. Unlike me, he was a good athlete, and he played sports long before he got into theater. His vernacular seemed to spring more from the ball field than the salon. Dad had a grizzled half-time approach when barking out stage notes: "Blocking! Blocking! Learn your blocking. . . . Lines people! Learn the damn lines. Master nuts and bolts, then we can move on from there." Sometimes dad issued compliments, but they were concise. His speaking style and approach to his craft were muscular, not flowery. "Good," he'd say, "Now you're getting it." Or, "That was tighter."

The students enjoyed pleasing this man of decisive certainty. He joked with students, but no one doubted who was in charge. Dad welcomed and encouraged suggestions, but he had final say on the merits of a suggestion. I admired the confidence and competence that my father exuded at those rehearsals.

Although I initially was afraid to try out for a play at my school, I realized that—after observing so many rehearsals, so many stage notes, such relentless tinkering with each line reading—I might have some grasp of the basics of my father's craft, and I decided to take a stab at it. I heeded his advice when preparing my audition; I had a line reading in mind for every sentence—how I would sound, how I would gesture, what direction I would cast my eyes. It may not have been the most spontaneous audition, but my willingness to craft a plan and then execute it compensated for my acne and awkwardness. That audition—for a play called *Inherit the Wind*—transformed my life in two ways.

First, my fear about actually performing notwithstanding, I realized that focusing on small steps was an effective way of achieving large, daunting, long-term goals. Laurence Olivier I'm not, but this method served me reasonably well, both in landing the lead in the play and in preparing for the role. In short, I learned to have confidence in the power of incremental improvement. This confidence has never left me and epitomizes the strategic approach that I espouse in this book.

Second, I played the role of Clarence Darrow. (Henry Drummond, the fictionalized character in the play, was Darrow through and through). Darrow battled in court the great fundamentalist champion William Jennings Bryan. The two clashed over the nature of religion, the meaning of Charles Darwin's work, the literal interpretation of the Bible, and the very existence of God.

My dad had long equated ministers, particularly fundamentalist ministers, with con men, so I was already a skeptic, but memorizing Darrow day in and day out had a long-standing effect on me. Darrow made connections between Darwin's work and America's Enlightenment history—our heritage of intellectual honesty and government based on reason not religious bias. Darrow expressed these views with zest and a sardonic wit that served a deep idealism. Darrow's proud agnosticism was convincing. I drank up Darrow, reading Irving Stone's biography of him and concluding, as I still do, that Darrow, whatever his personal shortcomings, was the greatest lawyer this world has known. I've had reasons to sometimes be disappointed in the law and those lawyers who stray from the highest ideals of the profession, but Clarence Darrow inspired me to pursue a law degree. I'm still thankful for that.

Yet the most resonant aspect of that play today is how differently our twenty-first-century world treats religious fundamentalism than did the world in 1955, when the play was written. The play was in part a parable about McCarthyism. The playwrights, Jerome Lawrence and Robert Edwin Lee, were protesting the injustices of the McCarthy era through the metaphor of the Scopes Trial. They were speaking out for intellectual freedom. An oversimplified summary of the play's message might be: "We shall rise above 1950s McCarthyism just as America rose above antiscientific 1920s fundamentalism."

But something funny happened on the way to progress. What was perceived in 1955 as a largely settled issue in mainstream American society (Darwin right, creationism wrong) has today become a controversy as strong as, in many ways stronger than, that which existed in the 1920s—in the America of spats and speakeasies. That controversy has spread beyond the single issue of creationism to pervade vast reaches of American public discourse. America, the nation of progress, has slipped backward in a way that, as we shall see, endangers the very nature of our Republic.

America changed, and dramatically so, as I moved into adulthood. My father, whose religion was more the Fighting Irish football team than the Roman Catholic Church, encouraged me to go to the University of Notre Dame. I did, and I'm glad I did. Despite my love of Darrow and his views, I saw that religion in general, and Catholicism in particular, could sometimes embody some very positive values.

Maryknoll nuns and priests fought for social justice in Latin America. I remember the brave sisters killed by the right-wing death squads in El Salvador (killed after being raped and tortured). Mario Cuomo and Robert Kennedy remain my heroes. Catholicism was different then—and was perceived differently then. The pedophilia scandals had yet to make headlines. Though I was not a Mass-going Catholic even at Notre Dame, I felt some cultural allegiance to Catholicism. Even today, I continue to harbor many positive feelings about it, particularly regarding my Irish-Catholic cultural heritage.

In 2009 there was a strong movement among conservative Catholics, including the president of the U.S. Conference of Catholic Bishops, to shun President Barack Obama as a commencement speaker at Notre Dame. This vocal affront to a sitting president, because he is prochoice, would never have occurred in earlier decades. For example, at my own Notre Dame graduation, Canadian prime minister Pierre Trudeau, who was prochoice and whose wife led a bohemian lifestyle, was welcomed to speak with very little controversy. Things were different then.

After college I joined the Jesuit Volunteer Corps in Alaska, another positive experience involving Catholicism. The organization specifically told us volunteers not to proselytize. The work was truly focused on social service. The idea of a twenty-two-year-old kid serving as a "house parent" for Native American teen boys who faced very serious personal issues (several of these boys were victims and, in some cases, perpetrators of dangerous crimes) was something for which I was completely unqualified. I learned a lot. The poverty and social strife I saw affected me for life. I thank the sense of mission within some elements of the Catholic Church for this valuable education, an experience that strengthened my commitment to social justice.

After law school I entered private practice and then served briefly as a state assistant attorney general in Maine, handling child-protection litigation cases, among others. In that position, I was exposed to even more social problems and injustice. I saw hideous cases of abuse, including child sexual abuse photos that made you hide your eyes. I eventually left the attorney general's office to run successfully for the Maine legislature.

During my years as an elected official, I started to witness the significant influence of fundamentalist and conservative religion on American law. I served ten years in the legislature, three of them on the judiciary committee, before which fundamentalist Christian and Catholic groups often testified. They lobbied the judiciary committee because they cared deeply about many of the issues within the committee's purview. The media often prominently covered the desires of these groups to deny a woman's right to choose and to discriminate based on sexual orientation, but I found that their interests were much wider than that. I did not agree with most of their positions on issues, though there were exceptions. I respected some of the social justice positions taken by some religious leaders, and I remember one brave priest from Bangor speaking out for equal rights for gay citizens, but I found many fundamentalist policy viewpoints to be disturbing.

I once took a call from a fundamentalist preacher regarding so-called parental consent. Some states have a law requiring all minor girls to get parental permission before they can have an abortion, and he advocated for such a law in Maine. I told the minister that I was confident most parents would be very caring if their minor daughter became pregnant but that some parents might react in a physically abusive way. I told the minister that for those girls who feared an abusive reaction to their pregnancy, the option of a consultation with a trained counselor would be an appropriate alternative.

I'll never forget the minister's response: "Well, sometimes the rod must be applied." And he, with accuracy, referenced a biblical passage to support his point. I felt stunned by the calm and, indeed, casual way with which he—a minister who preached to a congregation every Sunday—advocated hitting a pregnant child—a position fully consistent with his reading of scripture and his own religious "values."

This was a dramatic moment for me in two ways. First, I saw that my worldview, still strongly informed by the values of people like Darrow, was diametrically opposed to the values of this brand of religion. Second, it sank in how strong and confident this brand of religion was, even in a New

England state like Maine. I wondered to myself, if fundamentalism could be so extremely vocal, organized, and visible in the halls of my state legislature, what must it be like in Alabama?

I was later appointed to the appropriations committee and elected Majority Whip by my party colleagues. Between these two positions, which dealt with purse strings and leadership, respectively, I was again involved with the legislative issues important to the Christian fundamentalists. During these years, I became increasingly convinced that the views and positions of the fundamentalist Protestants from whom I heard, as well as the views and positions stemming from certain quarters within the Catholic Church, represented a fundamental rejection of the values that I—and the majority of Americans—held most dear. As a state legislator, I passionately advocated different policies, and I felt a desire to espouse the philosophy that drove them. At one point, I took an opportunity to strike a small blow for secular values—and to have some fun while doing so.

The Maine legislature, like most legislatures in America, opens with a prayer. This usually involves legislators scheduling clergy from their home districts to open the session. It's perceived as an honor and it gives clergy something to mention to their congregation at services ("I want to thank Representative Jones who asked me to open the session last Tuesday"). When things got too hectic or busy to extend formal invitations to clergy, legislators often asked one of their own to offer a quick prayer. I decided I'd put in my name for when the legislature needed someone to pinch hit. The day I was called, I offered a "prayer" that I liked: I quoted Walt Whitman and Susan Jacoby from her book *Freethinkers*. I heard a couple of grumbles from one or two people on the other side of the aisle, but I suffered no particular negative political consequence. Although offering the "prayer" was a hoot, at the time I knew of no organization, no strong lobbying force whatsoever for the secular values that I had communicated—Jeffersonian and Madisonian values.

In 2009, I read an article about the Secular Coalition for America. I'd never heard of it, but this organization, which lobbies, advocates, and organizes under the banner of our secular founding principles and our Constitution, seemed to embody the voice I wanted to see working in Washington, DC, on behalf of my own values. Learning that it was looking for an executive director, I applied for the position and was lucky to be chosen. I had lobbied for my state bar association years earlier and enjoyed it, but I'm particularly happy to do what I'm doing now. I'm glad to get up in the morning and look forward every day to working on issues that I care deeply about. I enjoy working for a cause rooted in our nation's proud heritage and very creation, when Americans boldly broke free from the stranglehold of theocratic government. It is an exciting job, encompassing both lobbying in Washington and coalition building throughout America.

I'm deeply passionate about our Coalition because its mission aligns fully with my personal vision of where our nation must go if we are to be true to the values of our Founders. Herb Silverman, founder and president of the Secular Coalition for America, had a historic vision in initiating and creating the Coalition (see appendix). We are a nonpartisan organization and we specifically seek participation from all those who support our mission—no matter their political stripes. Indeed, the Secular Coalition for America has not only many Democratic supporters but also Libertarian and Republican supporters. Given the fundamentalist tenor of the Republican Party today, the number of Republicans in our Coalition is smaller than I would like. We are determined to welcome as many people as are willing to join us.

In the most specific sense, the Secular Coalition for America fights for the separation of church and state, as well as for the acceptance and inclusion of Secular Americans in civic life. Those who hold the naturalistic worldview of Deists like Jefferson or Madison, or of agnostics like the charitable Warren Buffett and Bill Gates, or of atheists like the humanitarians Brad Pitt and Angelina Jolie, are all Secular Americans. All these people share a philosophy worthy of full inclusion in American political life. The Secular Coalition for America serves an essential patriotic mission. At a time when theocratic attitudes are on the march in America like never before and the all-important wall of separation between church and state is crumbling, Herb Silverman's brainchild strives to meet this pivotal moment in history and protect the secular nature of our government.

Despite this new, unified effort, the secular movement suffers from a noble flaw. Secular people tend to have an almost religious faith in statistics and dry arguments and abstractions as the proper method by which to carry the day. This has made it difficult to connect with the broader American public, particularly when many of our battles emphasize symbols—and not the numerous religious laws that harm real people.

Secular Americans remain a sleeping giant, a huge demographic that has thus far failed to flex its own muscle, much less galvanize the general population. We ignore people suffering under religious privilege while shaking our fist at a slapped-together manger with a plastic baby Jesus in the town square at Christmas time. While symbols are meaningful and these particular symbols on public grounds do violate Madison's Constitution, Secular Americans must do better to reach all Americans. We must explain the human story—the human harm and the outright abuse of our tax dollars that result from religious privileging in law.

Theocratic fundamentalists love when the debate is about nativity scenes or "the war on Christmas," because, meanwhile, that sideshow allows them the opportunity to quietly transform our government—and our laws—to their liking in ways that harm real people. If we are to be strategic, if we are to build a case to a broader audience—and we can—the secular movement must unite around the human harm caused by religious bias. A uniting call to compassion—and to moral outrage—makes smart strategy because it's so deeply just, and because it appeals to the best of our nature. An energized reaction to our message—to our very human stories—is in itself unique and new within the secular movement. We must stir people's emotions with a mission of justice and compassion, not merely for Secular American but for all Americans.

If our goal is to improve our world and serve our fellow human beings, then a savvier strategy, a more businesslike strategy, a strategy more accepting of the nature of human emotions, is imperative. Religious special rights are about real people and real harm. Secular Americans must offer sound arguments, but we must do so in a way that connects with the hearts of our fellow Americans. Now is the time to step forward and take moral responsibility for our nation through social action. After reading this book, I hope you will see the imperative of doing just that—and a clear course of action for us to return America to its secular roots.

1 Introduction

The Crumbled Wall between Church and State

I believe that God wants me to be president.

— George W. Bush

I contemplate with sovereign reverence that act of the whole American people which declared that their legislature should "make no law respecting establishment of religion or prohibiting the free exercise thereof," thus building a wall of separation between church and state.

— Thomas Jefferson

I was twelve, riding in the backseat of the family car on a vacation in the American West. I'd been given *The Children's Bible* as a gift. With time on my hands, I decided to read the Holy Scripture. The trip sure felt pretty biblical, what with dad driving us through the desert and all. I got to the part where God tells Abraham to kill his son. If Abraham was willing to kill his son, then, in God's eyes, Abraham was a moral person—a God-fearing person. I looked up at my dad in the driver's seat and wondered to myself how God fearing he might be out here in the desert.

This was the first time I remember having real questions about the Bible. Would a truly moral person obey such a command? Would a moral God issue such a command—even as a test of loyalty? Would it be moral to treat a child as something to be used as property—an object to be used as a religious sacrifice?

The story of Abraham is an ancient one. And we're living in what is often called the modern age. Surely the invocation of religion today would never place children at risk, right? Well, let's consider a true story from the twenty-first century.

Amiyah White, age two, attended a child-care center in Alabama. The center's staff lost track of Amiyah and she was left alone, trapped in a van. After two hours in that van under the Alabama sun, Amiyah's two-year-old heart gave out, and she died alone in that van. On the outside of the van were painted the words "Holy Church." Amiyah attended a religious child-care center. Now, you might say, Amiyah's death was an accident that also could have happened in a secular child-care center. True, but such an event would be less likely to happen—because under Alabama law, health and safety statutes that apply to secular child-care centers do not apply to religious child-care centers. As the head of the Alabama Christian Coalition said, "The pastors and the congregations are our quality control."

Let's consider for a moment this "quality control." Under Alabama law, (1) secular child-care centers must keep medications locked up, while religious child-care centers are exempt from medication-safety regulations; (2) secular child-care centers must follow food-safety regulations, while religious child-care centers are exempt from food-safety regulations; (3) secular child-care centers must submit to unannounced state inspections, while religious child-care centers are exempt from such inspections; (4) secular child-care centers must obey child-staff ratio laws, while religious child-care centers need not obey child-staff ratio laws; (5) secular child-care providers must participate in safety training that, for example, covers proper child tracking, while providers at religious child-care centers are exempt from such training.

Was Amiyah's death an anomaly? Perhaps. And yet a three-year-old named DeMyreon Lindley, who attended a different religious child-care center in Alabama, was left alone in his center's van for ten hours before he died.

No politician, in the context of Alabama child-care laws, has argued that it is a positive characteristic to actually consider killing a child at the behest of a deity. But Alabama law is similar to the story of Abraham in this respect: they both share the concept that religion justifies a separate moral code. Put another way, by providing an exemption to a basic code of safety simply because a business invokes religion, modern Alabama law stands united with the tribal Abrahamic code in its willingness to endanger children in the name of religion. While Alabama law is particularly extreme, there are more than ten states that provide for some form of religious exemption from laws governing child-care centers.

Now consider a religious practice of the Incas from five hundred years ago. The Incas would take children to the mountains, drug them, then kill them as a sacrifice to their gods. That was part of their Pre-Columbian religion. Primitive? Perhaps. Brutal? No doubt. But at least they tried to anesthetize the children and killed them swiftly. Contrast that with what happens in twenty-first-century America.

Jessica Crank was fifteen when a tumor began to grow on her shoulder. The tumor was treatable with modern medical science, but Jessica's mother did not believe in modern medical science. She treated her child with the Epistle of James. Had a secular parent neglected his or her child's medical needs, the law would have unequivocally authorized the government to remove the endangered child for proper medical care. Jessica's mother and her pastor could correctly point to the "faith-healing" exemption in Tennessee's child-protection law as providing their actions with wider latitude. Jessica's tumor grew and grew until it was the size of a basketball. Jessica suffered extended, agonizing pain—then she died.

In so-called faith-healing homes, children with otherwise treatable maladies have needlessly vomited fecal matter, bled from giant eye tumors, and gasped for water as a result of untreated diabetes. And, yes, children have died and continue to die in agonizing torture. It is unconscionable that, in most states, there are so-called faith-healing exemptions to basic child-protection law.

Many Americans, including perhaps readers of this book, protested or spoke out against the U.S government's use of waterboarding. As bad as waterboarding is, waterboarding usually does not lead to permanent injury and is rarely fatal. Compare waterboarding to what happened to—and what continues to happen to—these innocent children: Vomiting fecal matter? Bleeding from eyes? Tumors on children so festering and large that people, even at a distance, gag from the smell? All this needless and pointless suffering, often followed by death?

The fact that fanatical parents may not recognize their own actions as torture does not by one iota diminish the torture that these children experience. This torture of children, justified on religious grounds, is worse than anything that occurred in Guantanamo or Abu Ghraib. Yet, relatively speaking, there is not a peep of protest. Following his election, President Barack Obama proclaimed, "Waterboarding violates our ideals and our values. I do believe that it's torture." When will the same be said about the torture of innocent American children that is justified in the name of religion?

This legal imprimatur for "faith healing" violates the very nature of our form of government, and the separation of church and state. The statutes used to excuse these actions give the stamp of "morality" to immoral actions. This "moral" stamp results from the concerted efforts of religious extremists.

The Fundamentalist-Industrial Complex

The hideous deaths of Amiyah White, DeMyreon Lindley, and Jessica Crank represent human horror stories. But they also represent something much more insidious. Their deaths, and the deaths of all other children as a result of laws that privilege religion, are emblematic of a much broader violation of—and attack on—the secular values of our Founders and our Constitution. As John Witte of the Center for the Study of Law and Religions at Emory University states, "Separation of church and state is no longer the law of the land." This change has gone largely unnoticed by the media and the American public in general.

You will hear Rush Limbaugh complain about "special rights." Fundamentalists tell us to fear the specter of special rights for gay citizens, though of course gay Americans aren't after special rights—merely equal rights. The irony is that special rights actually do exist in this country—for religious groups. Just as the described horrors suffered by children have all occurred under some form of legal imprimatur, some statutory form of recognition, so too have countless other injustices and instances of harm been authorized by many other forms of religious bias inscribed in law. These laws aren't unenforced blue laws from the time of the Salem witch trials. They are laws that grant special rights in twenty-first-century America to religion and that are justifed by ancient texts.

There is no comparison between calls for basic equal rights among all Americans no matter one's gender, sexual orientation, race, or religion and laws that elevate one class of people over another on the basis of religion. Rush Limbaugh would likely point to affirmative action as "special rights." Yet whether one agrees or disagrees with affirmative action, one must concede that, in the case of African-Americans, centuries of slavery and many decades of violations of civil rights constitute a reasonable argument for it. What similar historical injustices or disadvantages have religious groups in the United States suffered to justify the special status they enjoy in law today? Why give people like Billy Graham, Rick Warren, and Ted Haggard affirmative action for religious affiliation?

You might be asking, surely Billy Graham's multimillion dollar organization doesn't get special rights, does it? This would be the Billy Graham who complained to Richard Nixon of "synagogues of Satan" and who, encouraging a militaristic policy during the Vietnam War, quoted Jesus as saying, "I am come to send fire on earth" (Luke 12:49) and "I am come not to send peace but a sword" (Matthew 10:34–36). Billy Graham may be retired, but yes, his multimillion dollar organization, now run by his son, Franklin Graham, gets special legal rights that average businesses do not.

Surely Rick Warren doesn't get special rights, does he? This would be the Rick Warren who preached at Obama's inauguration and who, commenting on the famous Florida legal battle over Terri Schiavo (the woman who had been in a persistent vegetative state), compared her husband to a Nazi. Preacher Rick Warren is worth something approaching $10 million. Yes, Warren and his organization benefit from special legal rights.

Surely Ted Haggard's former organization doesn't get special rights, does it? You remember Ted Haggard, the Colorado Springs megaminister who preached against gay sex while having gay sex jacked up on meth. His former organization still controls many millions. Yes, religious organizations like his old one get special rights.

What types of special rights do these individuals and groups enjoy? To begin, nonprofit organizations must apply for tax-exempt status; religious groups are tax exempt by a less rigorous assertion of religious status. Nonprofits get audited by the IRS whenever the IRS chooses; churches are not audited without a special IRS decision.

Perhaps more insidiously, religions enjoy legal privileges that corrode our most basic American values. In most states, religious groups can say in one of their child-care centers: "You're a Jew? You're fired." Similarly, in one of their charitable organizations, they can say to the administrative assistant or janitor: "You're gay? You're fired." This is true even in states that generally prohibit discrimination based on sexual orientation. You're agnostic like Albert Einstein? Fired. You're atheist like Brad Pitt? Fired.

These same businesses, like the ones run by megachurches, can exempt themselves from many land-use laws other businesses must obey because federal politicians chose to exempt religious organizations from those laws in the 1990s.

Where's the investigative journalism on the scandals I've described above? Pat Robertson said that he believes Jesus is currently the Lord of government, business, and education and wants his version of Jesus to be the "Lord of the press." Robertson needn't be concerned, because religious ideologies and bias are too often treated with kid gloves in the media.

Although I like to think this is not the case, there is a tendency in journalistic writing to treat religion with timid deference, even when the situations or public conduct would otherwise set off alarm bells for reporters in any nonreligious context. This timidity is so pervasive it is sometimes hard to notice. In a February 2, 2011, *New York Times* article, for example, a Muslim religious leader in Afghanistan was depicted rather like a moderate because he favored stoning with small stones rather than big stones as punishment for sexual activity. In any other context, the big-stone versus small-stone barbarism would be unequivocally labeled as such, but, when it comes to religion, reporters back gingerly away, swaddling even the most extreme statements in words like "faith."

But fundamentalist Muslims have no real political clout in America. No, the real political power is held by fundamentalist Christians. Give Christian fundamentalists their due. They organize. They meet. Their supporters give money to the cause. And they have been hugely effective in electing their own. Indeed, at no prior time in American history have so many politicians with such expressly theocratic views held high public office.

Here's a sampling: Congressman Tim Walberg, who chairs the workforce protection committee, which oversees labor laws, embodies much of what America has become in the twenty-first century. Congressman Walberg is the one who objected to a law prohibiting discrimination based on religion within Head Start programs because of his concerns about the threat posed by Wiccans and Muslims. Senator Marco Rubio embodies our times too. He has dismissed Jefferson's "wall of separation of church and state" and supports teaching creationism in school. Then there's Congressman Ralph Hall, chair of the science and technology committee, who has worked to undermine *science*. These and other like-minded politicians are not on the fringe. They are at the center of power in America today, and they do not represent the judicious views of Jefferson or Madison.

The Strategy, the Plan, the Vision
In mid-twentieth-century America, rationalism and separation of church and state were ascendant. The playwrights who penned *Inherit the Wind* expressed the clear majority view. John Kennedy, the strongest advocate of separation of church and state since Madison, was highly popular. What happened?

Churches have always been powerful and influential in this country, but in this century many individual churches are major business enterprises, boasting child-care centers, ice cream parlors, addiction treatment centers, fitness clubs, broadcasting facilities, and powerful lobbying enterprises, often with a proselytizing mission. Special rights for religion create a largely unregulated, separate business universe that leads only to more special rights for these increasingly powerful organizations. As a result, religious groups experience very little oversight of their statutorily created special rights.

This book is meant to create awareness about the damage that is being done to our country and to our Constitution in the name of religion, and to offer a plan to do something about it. This book calls upon Secular Americans and all Americans of good will to participate in returning America to its true secular heritage, to the ideals of Madison and of Jefferson. In chapters 2 and 3, it provides an overview of the most basic principles of our Founders—the heritage that we must reinvigorate. The book will not only show how theocratic laws are destroying our country's secular heritage, but also discuss the myriad ways in which our present descent toward theocracy and the privileging of religion in law unjustly harms us all in multiple ways.

Chapter 4 examines how a bizarre, unhealthy, and theocratic attitude toward sex has undermined the rights of women and sexual minorities, and has made sexual trivia an insidiously central focus in American life and politics. Chapter 5 juxtaposes the great dueling American traditions of religious hucksterism and scientific innovation and entrepreneurship. These two traditions offer a defining choice regarding the future of our Republic.

Chapters 6 and 7 contrast the unprecedented number of theocratic politicians in high elective office today and their worldviews with those who speak for the traditions of people like Jefferson, Madison, and Darrow. Chapter 8 describes the dramatic growth of the secular demographic despite the still pervasive power of theocrats in America.

Chapter 9 presents my plan for returning America to its secular heritage, and chapter 10 presents a vision of what a secular America will look like once we return to the heritage of our founding. It's a vision of a patriotic, secular government informed by strong moral values.

As will be made clear in this book, I believe in flag and country. I believe in the values of our nation's founders. That is why I am a Secular American. It is the patriotic duty of all Americans to stop fundamentalist extremists from controlling our laws. Sadly, they have been effective at doing just that. The intent of this book is to demonstrate that the theocratic attack on America is real, to expose theocratic injustices that should be of concern to all Americans, and to offer a strategy for rejuvenating America's patriotic secular heritage.

2 Our Secular Heritage
One Nation under the Constitution

I think we should keep this clean, keep it simple, go back to what our founders and our founding documents meant. They're quite clear that we would create law based on the God of the Bible and the Ten Commandments. It's pretty simple.

—Sarah Palin

Although the detail of the formation of the American governments is at present little known or regarded either in Europe or in America, it may hereafter become an object of curiosity. It will never be pretended that any persons employed in that service had interviews with the gods, or were in any degree under the influence of Heaven . . . it will forever be acknowledged that these governments were contrived merely by the use of reason and the senses.

—John Adams

In recent years we've heard a lot about "American exceptionalism," the idea that America's place in world history is not only unique but also uniquely positive. To many on the Theocratic Right, the concept carries with it a divine element. When asked about the idea of "American exceptionalism" in April 2009, President Barack Obama responded, "I believe in American exceptionalism, just as I suspect that the Brits believe in British exceptionalism and the Greeks believe in Greek exceptionalism." Although Sarah Palin and others attacked Obama for not being forceful enough in support of this concept, President Obama wisely avoided interpreting American exceptionalism through a jingoistic or theocratic lens.

That said, one can find Palin jingoistic and theocratic and still embrace the concept of American exceptionalism. I do. The exceptional nature of

American civil liberties and the enshrining of minority rights in our Constitution do indeed make the place of our nation in world history distinctly valuable and praiseworthy.

The separation of church and state, enshrined in our First Amendment, is central to America's unique and unprecedented civil liberties. While I fully admire and recognize the many vitally important individual liberties protected by our Constitution, I agree with the importance and emphasis that Thomas Jefferson placed on this foremost principle.

Jefferson directed that his three most important accomplishments be engraved on his headstone. Serving as President of the United States didn't make his cut, but his authoring of the Declaration of Independence, his fathering of the University of Virginia, and his crafting of the Virginia Statute for Religious Freedom did. The Virginia Statute for Religious Freedom served as the basis of the separation of church and state in our Constitution. That separation remained central to Jefferson's values—and is central to American exceptionalism. Had Jefferson consulted me, I might have suggested chiseling his stellar presidency on the gravestone, but Jefferson had a point. There have already been more than forty U.S. presidents, but the separation of church and state stands out as a singularly brilliant accomplishment in human history. And we have Jefferson and Madison (Jefferson's key collaborator) to thank for this world-changing concept.

Jefferson's "wall of separation between church and state" created one of the great steps forward for rational thought and civil discourse. Like the invention of the wheel, Jefferson's wall made not only our country but also our world a better place. Thus, when Ms. Palin and other theocrats focus on American exceptionalism in the divine sense and propose or adopt policies based on their particular interpretation of scripture rather than our Constitution, they in fact undermine that which truly makes America exceptional.

The Political Price of Independent Thought

The Washington Monument and the Jefferson Memorial stand steps from each other on the National Mall in Washington, DC, and Washington's Mt. Vernon and Jefferson's Monticello remain the two most visited presidential homes. These sites symbolize the tremendous pride we feel in our nation's founding, but what kind of nation are we today in comparison to the days of our nation's birth?

Let's engage in a little mind experiment. Let us pretend that we are political consultants. Let us assume a young politician preparing to run for

Congress enters our consulting firm. How will we help this candidate? As Majority Whip of my legislature, I helped recruit candidates. A smart first step is to vet candidates. Google the heck out of them. See what they might have said that the opposition will inevitably dig up.

What would we advise an aspiring politician if we were to uncover that he'd made these statements on Facebook:

Quote one: "The hocus-pocus phantasm of a god like another Cerberus with one body and three heads had its birth and growth in the blood of thousands and thousands of martyrs."

Quote two: The clergy dreads "the advance of science as witches do the approach of daylight."

Quote three: The candidate hopes that "the human mind will get back to the freedom it enjoyed 2,000 years ago"—that is, before the advent of Christianity.

Quote four: "Religions are all alike—founded upon fables and mythologies."

Quote five: "I do not find in orthodox Christianity one redeeming feature."

Quote six: Christianity is "our particular superstition."

In the real world of politics, how would we political consultants advise this aspiring candidate? Having spent ten years in elective office, I'll tell you what we'd say, "Sorry, Thomas Jefferson. Have you considered accounting?" Then we'd say, "That'll be $5,000 for our consulting fee." Any one of the above quotes would land a candidate today in boiling hot water, but all six quotes are Jefferson's.

Just imagine, Thomas Jefferson, one of our greatest thinkers, one of our greatest presidents, might be lost to us if he ran for office today—because the author of the Declaration of Independence dared to think independently.

Particularly in the last three decades, a candidate of Jefferson's views would face almost insurmountable electoral odds. Consider the words of W. A. Criswell, the man selected by President Ronald Reagan to deliver the benediction for the 1984 Republican National Convention. Criswell said the separation of church and state "is the figment of some infidel's imagination." It was Criswell who introduced Reagan at a giant gathering of fundamentalist preachers in 1980 to whom Reagan made this pivotal declaration: "I know you can't endorse me, but . . . I want you to know that I endorse you."

Now what if we political consultants uncovered the following set of quotes from another aspiring politician:

> *Quote one:* "In no instance have . . . the churches been guardians of the liberties of the people."

> *Quote two:* "Religious bondage shackles and debilitates the mind and unfits it for every noble enterprise."

> *Quote three:* "During almost 15 centuries has the legal establishment of Christianity been on trial. What has been its fruits? More or less, in all places, pride and indolence in the clergy; ignorance and servility in the laity; in both, superstition, bigotry, and persecution."

> *Quote four:* "Religion . . . has been much oftener a motive to repression than a restraint from it."

How might political consultants react to a candidate with the above quotes? As with Jefferson, the response would likely be, "Hang it up there, James Madison, Father of the Constitution."

At least Jefferson looked like a politician: he was tall, handsome, and even played the violin. Madison was short, paunchy, and shaped rather like an oversize toad, and is one of the most underrated of the Founders. But if the words and ideals of Jefferson cause today's theocrats fits, Madison's might put theocrats into an outright seizure.

Jefferson famously wrote the words "separation of church and state." Madison wrote that government and religion are served by "the *total* separation of church and state." (emphasis added) As a twenty-five-year-old legislator, Madison succeeded in his first major legislative proposal, which left religious opinion completely to the "dictates of conscience."

Many secularists have seemed pleased simply because President Obama has made less of a show of the National Prayer Breakfast than had President George W. Bush. Contrast that with Madison, who publicly opposed any government-sponsored prayer day. In 1817 he wrote that a national day of prayer would "imply and certainly nourish the erroneous idea of a national religion."

Today a chaplain opens Congress with a prayer. Madison said, "Establishment of a chaplainship to Congress is a . . . violation of equal rights, as well as . . . Constitutional principles." As the Constitution's prime author, he'd know.

With regard to chaplains in the military, Madison said, "Better also to disarm in the same way, the precedent of chaplainship for the army and navy than erect them into a political authority in matters of religion." Madison concluded that the appointment of military chaplains would inevitably constitute majority tyranny—that religious truth would be tested by numbers and that major sects would end up governing minor sects. This, as Madison foresaw and we shall see later, is the case today.

What of so-called faith-based initiatives? Madison opposed federal recognition of religious charities, even when they involved no federal funds. According to the Father of the Constitution, a bill vesting in churches an authority to provide for the support of the poor was something he opposed as giving "legal agency in carrying into effect a public and civil duty." Today, so-called faith-based initiatives involve your tax dollars going to religious organizations. But get this: Madison vetoed legislation that recognized a church charity even though the legislation gave the church no money at all.

Regarding legislation pertaining to a parcel of land for the Baptist Church, Madison opposed "the appropriation of funds of the U.S. for the use and support of religious societies," which he saw as contrary to the Establishment Clause of the First Amendment. He not only vetoed bills that would have allocated surplus land for churches but also vetoed bills that offered only symbolic support to houses of worship. Wrote Madison: "There is an evil which ought to be guarded against in the indefinite accumulation of property . . . by ecclesiastical corporations."

In other words, Madison went much further than any recent president in separating government from religion. Many fundamentalists mouth the phrase "original intent." I'm quoting the real original intent, from the Father of the Constitution. It is understandable that theocrats seek to paper over Madison, and even delete references to Jefferson in textbooks, as was recently attempted in Texas.

The forceful nature of Madison's strong support of church-state separation is something fundamentalists work hard to shout over. They must shout because, despite their repetitive claims, America was not founded as a Christian nation—the evidence against them is the decisive clarity of the *actual* original intent. In his day, Jefferson espoused legislation in Virginia that specifically rejected the idea of Christian-only religious protection to include, according to Jefferson himself, protections for "the Jew," "the Hindoo," "the Mahometan," and "the infidel." Jefferson won the 1800 election over strong opposition from most religious groups. How? Well, by one estimate, only 10–15 percent of Americans were church members in 1800.

Some say Jefferson was a Christian. Perhaps, but Jefferson, in writing, specifically rejected the following: the resurrection, the miracles, Christ's divinity, and the immaculate conception. Can you imagine what fundamentalists would say about such a "Christian" today?

Jefferson proposed the idea for the Virginia Statute for Religious Freedom in 1776 at the same time he met Madison, with whom he would have a political partnership lasting a half century. Madison, as a legislator, led the statute to passage in 1786, stating that no one "shall be compelled to . . . support any religious worship . . . *whatsoever*" and that one's religious opinion "shall in no wise diminish, *enlarge, or affect* their civil capacities." (emphasis added)

Let's give John Adams, our most religious early president, final word on whether America is a Christian nation. "The United States," Adams wrote, marks "the example of governments erected on the simple principles of nature. . . . Governments thus founded on the natural authority of the people alone without a pretense of miracle or mystery . . . are a great point gained in the favor of the rights of mankind."

The 1796–1797 treaty between the United States and Tripoli, reviewed and approved by the secretary of state, unanimously approved by the Senate, and signed by President John Adams, states that the U.S. government is "not, in any sense, founded on the Christian religion." *Not in any sense.* The treaty was drafted under the previous administration, and the language was specifically approved by President George Washington.

Washington, Adams, Jefferson, Madison—these were leaders of the Enlightenment. Just as important, they were thinkers imbued with Enlightenment values. Sometimes this made them lightning rods—an especially apt metaphor when recalling that clergy in both America and Britain condemned Ben Franklin's lightning rod as a sacrilegious defiance of God's ability to smite whosoever God chose. But that view, so similar to the attitudes of today's fundamentalists, was a minority view during America's founding. Jefferson, widely accused (with some justification) of apostasy, won elections and remained revered by the solid majority of Americans.

JFK, Dr. King, and School Prayer
In the 1800s America saw a rise in fundamentalism. By one estimate the percentage of church-going Americans doubled from 1776 to 1832, from 17 percent to approximately 34 percent. The times became riskier for freethinking

politicians such as the one who said this: "The Bible is not my book nor Christianity my profession. I could never give assent to the long, complicated statements of Christian dogma." This freethinking politician was Abraham Lincoln, who never joined a church and who, according to his best friend and law partner, "died an unbeliever." Maybe Lincoln's law partner was wrong. Maybe Lincoln, who was well versed in the Bible, was really religious, but had the Savior of the Union faced his own words today, his political career would probably stop short of Congress, much less the presidency.

Just maybe we should include freethinkers in public debate: take, for example, the great feminist Elizabeth Cady Stanton, "The Bible and the Church have been the greatest stumbling blocks in the way of women's emancipation." Stanton also said, "I know of no other book that so fully teaches the subjection and degradation of women."

Stanton may have been thinking of Ephesians 5:24: "As the church is subject to Christ, so let the wives be to their own husbands in every thing." Or perhaps First Corinthians 11:9, which says that woman was "made from man and for man." When fundamentalists point to the Bible to support the view that women are to be subordinate, they are justified—if you accept the premise that the Bible is worthy of greater deference than any other document. As the experts tell us, the Bible has gone through so many convoluted changes, redrafts, and translations that, even if one accepts biblical inerrancy, the question remains: which Bible? We'll leave that debate to the experts and turn instead to the Lincoln of American letters: Mark Twain.

Ernest Hemingway wrote that "all modern American literature comes from one book, *Huckleberry Finn* by Mark Twain." *Huckleberry Finn* is widely proclaimed the great American novel. What is the central conflict of that novel? Morality, as laid down by the church, requires that Huck turn in Jim, the runaway slave. Huck accepts as gospel that helping Jim is immoral—against God. To help his friend, Huck, believing clear church teaching, chooses the fires of hell. Author Mark Twain is no less clear than the church in presenting his views: "If there is a God, he is a malign thug."

Twain also wrote, "I cannot see how a man of any large degree of humorous perception can ever be religious—unless he purposely shuts the eyes of his mind and keeps them shut by force." There was a time when America believed that a person with Mark Twain's views on religion should be included as an equal part of the American tapestry.

The chain of open skeptics and freethinkers continues from Walt Whitman to Thomas Edison to Andrew Carnegie to Clarence Darrow. Inspiring people all, and all central to the American story. They must be included as equal voices in American life.

One person who thought this group should be included was John F. Kennedy. President Kennedy was more clear on separation of church and state than any president since Madison. "The separation of church and state is absolute," Kennedy said. "[America is] . . . where every man has the same right to attend or not attend the church of his choice."

In more recent years, a nun who served as a parochial school administrator said publicly at a conference that when a child enters a parochial school, they leave any constitutional right at the door. She said, if you want those constitutional rights, "you will have to leave." Court rulings support her view that private religious schools have far more leeway to restrict students than do public schools, but Kennedy was clear: "No church or church school is granted any public funds or political preference"—zero tax dollars for such religious schools. Religious schools have expelled students with AIDS and expelled students who were not sufficiently religious. Some religious schools refuse to offer special education. Such neglect and discrimination is not an option available to public schools. Federal law requires just treatment of children with mental disabilities. Public schools must accept all comers. Not so religious schools.

Kennedy's policies contrast with the America of recent decades, in which private religious schools receive tax dollars through textbook aid, vouchers, and transportation subsidies—yet they remain free from most state and federal regulations. The Golden Christian School in Cleveland had a curriculum based exclusively on watching videos. This religious school got your tax money. Another religious school hired a convicted murderer and had no fire alarms. That religious school got your tax money, too.

Kennedy's view was the mainstream view, both in his era and throughout most of America's history. He encouraged acceptance of the 1962 Supreme Court decision that prohibited government-run prayer in schools. Fundamentalists argued that the ruling "banned" prayer in school when in fact individual children were quite free to pray. The court simply said the government can't orchestrate school prayer. The 1962 decision left that choice to children and their families. It's called freedom.

One of the greatest Supreme Court justices in American history, William Brennan, like Kennedy, was a Catholic. Brennan put it best about schools and religion: "Families entrust public schools with the education of their children, but condition their trust on the understanding that the classroom will not purposefully be used to advance religious views that may conflict with the private beliefs of the student and their family." Religion and publicly funded schools do not mix well.

Politics and religion do mix in that each of us is, like Dr. Martin Luther King, entirely welcome to bring our values, religious or not, to any debate. Yet it was Dr. King who said of school-sponsored prayer: "It would be better if the school day began with a reading of the Bill of Rights rather than the Bible."

The Seductive Simplicity of Certainty

Thomas Jefferson believed that "reason and free inquiry are the only effectual agents against error." The Enlightenment philosophy of our Founders got enshrined in our Constitution, which indeed constitutes a philosophy, a worldview. This worldview stands inherently and most essentially as evidence based. Contrast this Enlightenment philosophy with that of George Hensley, a Pentecostal preacher who, like many religious people, passionately adhered to selected portions of the Bible's vast and contradictory texts. Hensley focused on Mark 16:18, which asserts the power to "take up serpents" and "drink any deadly thing," because "it shall not hurt them." This great theologian, George Hensley, died in 1955 of a snakebite. Hensley has thousands of followers to this day. His passionate preaching, like that of so many itinerant preachers, is part of a very significant American tradition, a tradition that stands in direct contrast to the views of our Founders. Back in Maine I found delicious irony in the fact that fundamentalists passionately pointed to those biblical passages condemning homosexuality, yet never mentioned the prohibition on eating shellfish, a biblical edict that would be none too helpful to Maine's emblematic lobster industry.

This à la carte reading of ancient texts is not unique to Christians. Osama bin Laden acted far more viciously than any viper, and certainly more viciously than Hensley. Yet, like George Hensley, bin Laden preached his selected scripture adamantly. I prefer the many religious people who purposely avert their eyes from the texts of their own scripture. Better to avert one's eyes than believe, especially when scripture exhorts people to violence and endangerment.

Just because I share a Jeffersonian skepticism about biblical literalism, I nonetheless assert that, by all means, the Bible should be required reading for public school children.

Read Luke 19:27, where Jesus is quoted as saying: "But those mine enemies, which would not that I should reign over them, bring them hither, and slay them before me." Read the Koran, too: "The unbelievers are your inveterate enemies." Then read the Constitution of the United States. Which of these documents evolves? Which of them proclaim themselves perfect and unchangeable?

When considering the sagacity of the Founders, remember that, in this century, women have been stripped, raped, and set on fire in the name of religion. Not in some ancient time. In this century, a pregnant woman has been cut open and her fetus impaled on a pike in the name of religion. In this century, two hundred men and women were hacked by machetes and burned alive in Nigeria—because women planned to wear bikinis! In 2002 in Saudi Arabia, fourteen girls burned to death in their school. Why? The country's "religious police" blocked the schoolgirls from exiting their burning school building and blocked rescue workers from entering because the girls weren't wearing proper Islamic dress! I completely disagree with those who stigmatize Muslims as a group, but we should also face unflinchingly the extremist and violent actions taken in the name of Islam.

Think of all the hours that could be spent helping others that are now spent explaining why we should agree with, or simultaneously embrace or ignore, harsh sexual codes from ancient Middle Eastern peoples, regardless of whether those ancient sects adhered to the Old Testament, the New Testament, or the Koran.

St. Augustine wrote that torture was an acceptable sanction for breaking the laws of men and, therefore, it was an acceptable sanction for breaking the laws of God. Hitler was never excommunicated, but Galileo was. The Catholic Church only recently recanted Galileo's excommunication. No word yet on booting Hitler from the fold.

One of our present Supreme Court justices, Antonin Scalia, who was appointed by Ronald Reagan, said, "The more Christian a country is the less likely it is to regard the death penalty as immoral." Perhaps he's right. Justice Scalia's principle might also be applied to Muslim fundamentalist countries. In a world where fundamentalism is on the rise, America must be made safe for the ideas of Einstein and Twain. Politics must be made safe for the ideas of Madison and Jefferson.

Let us follow two "golden rules":

First: "Do not to your neighbor what you would take ill from him." Jesus you might think? Too recent. Pittacus, the Greek sage—who lived more than five centuries before Christ (c. 640–568 BCE)

Second: Officials "shall be bound . . . to support the Constitution; but no religious test shall ever be required as a qualification to any office or public trust under the United States." This comes from our Constitution—in particular, Article 6, Section 3.

Our Constitution beautifully embraces the theory of evolution—societal evolution. As Jefferson said, "I am not an advocate for frequent changes in laws and constitutions, but laws and institutions must go hand in hand with the progress of the human mind. As that becomes more developed, more enlightened, as new discoveries are made, new truths discovered and manners and opinions change, with the change of circumstances, institutions must advance also to keep pace with the times."

The Bible and the Koran reject evolution, not just in the scientific sense, but in the humanistic sense. The words of the Bible and Koran are unchangeable, no matter what compassion, science, or thousands of years of reason may reveal. Blacks? Women? Gay people? Too bad. Your applications were received centuries too late. The Constitution—and this was Madison's original intent—is an evolutionary document by design. Madison's genius was his humble belief that what he knew in the late 1700s wasn't all there was to know and therefore our system must adapt and change.

Darwin and Einstein offered real books of revelation, profoundly new to our eyes—elegantly explaining marvelous rules of our universe. Just as surely, just as dramatically, and just as importantly, Madison revealed new and marvelous rules for human interactions. Just as Einstein showed us that light bends, Madison showed us that the light of justice bends in beautiful and unexpected ways—toward compassion and justice. Our world is all the more marvelous for it. In both Madison's and Einstein's case, we see an ennobling sense of humbleness to their brilliant revelations. Einstein said, "I prefer an attitude of humility corresponding to the weakness of our intellectual understanding of nature and of our own being."

The minds of Einstein and Madison make me very optimistic about the future. The trends arc toward science and compassion, inherently humble concepts, and, especially among the young, toward justice, secularism, and greater inclusion. However, those with the greatest and most absolute certainty can, at least at first, have a rhetorical advantage. Some people find certainty extremely comforting. Indeed, the seductive simplicity of certainty is the greatest rhetorical advantage of fundamentalism.

Let's give credit to fundamentalists. They sell the comfort of certainty, and many people have been buying, including our politicians. The Christian fundamentalists have secured special rights in Congress and the states. Fundamentalists have secured billions of tax dollars that are in turn used to help them achieve their political ends.

Almost thirty years ago fundamentalist author Robert Simonds wrote *How to Elect Christians to Public Office*. Dismissing the fundamentalists as mere crackpots was not savvy politics. Their strategy was excellent and successful beyond what their numbers would warrant. Can nonfundamentalist Americans—those committed to the separation of church and state—be as committed to truth as fundamentalists can be committed to unbending, ancient documents? Can we be as committed to gentleness as they are committed to corporal punishment in school? Can we be as committed to justice and inclusion as they are to judgmental harshness? Can we be as committed to action based on reason as they are to action based on unbending doctrine?

Perhaps the biggest motivation for action is the stark and harsh results of privileging of religion in U.S. law. We will see that, far from an intellectual abstraction, this breach of Jefferson's wall has greatly harmed Americans and people the world over. Moreover, fundamentalists, through their political and legislative efforts, have harmed the very American exceptionalism they claim to revere. After all, America is exceptional only so long as it embodies the rationalism and reason that were central to the genius of Jefferson and Madison, our brilliant leaders who envisioned, designed, and then built the all-important wall separating church and state.

3 Religious Bias in Law Harms Us All

Our greatness would not long endure without judges who respect the foundation of faith upon which our Constitution rests.

—Mitt Romney

During almost fifteen centuries has the legal establishment of Christianity been on trial. What has been its fruits? More or less in all places, pride and indolence in the clergy, ignorance and servility in the laity; in both, superstition, bigotry, and persecution.

—James Madison

You've heard the phrase "you can't legislate morality." In fact, the only thing you can legislate is morality. Legislative decisions embody the moral choices of a society. Most religious people are good and honorable citizens who place a high premium on morality, as they should, yet theocrats increasingly manipulate our laws and tax dollars in ways that harm real people—and that are, put simply, immoral.

Religious people will often ask the nonreligious, how can you be moral if you don't believe in God? Consider the words of Jefferson: "Fix Reason firmly in her seat. . . . Question with boldness even the existence of a God. . . . Do not be frightened from this enquiry by any fear of its consequences. If it end in a belief that there is no God, you will find incitements to virtue in the comfort and pleasantness you feel in its exercise and in the love of others which it will procure for you." I ask, how can our morals be rigidly bound by ancient texts rather than guided and modified by reason and compassion?

Whether we turn our attention to health care, the care of children, women's rights, tax policy, or general issues of religious discrimination, we see myriad examples of real people harmed by religious bias in law—

in short, by religious "morality." Yet the vast majority of Americans, including Americans, religious and secular, who care about separation of church and state, remain blithely unaware of even the most harmful and immoral of these laws.

You've already been briefly introduced to the horrific ways in which religious bias in law harms children, and we will see more examples of how it harms children, which is but one of several areas in American law that reeks with unjust bias. We must shine a light on the many ways that religious bias in law and in many of our government institutions harms all of us and, through our foreign policy, harms people the world over.

Religious Bias Hurts Our Men and Women in Uniform

Federal law requires everyone who enlists in the Armed Forces to take the enlistment oath, pledging to support and defend the U.S. Constitution. The Constitution states that religion cannot be used as a qualification for public service and that our government can neither advance nor inhibit religion. Despite this oath, assignments and promotions based on religious membership rather than merit have occurred in the U.S. military, as have direct endorsements of religion, particularly in recent decades. The military has failed to create effective mechanisms for reporting and, when necessary, disciplining those who discriminate and harass based on religion.

In 2004 "friendly fire" killed Pat Tillman, who left the National Football League to join the Army Rangers. The circumstances of his being shot in the head three times by U.S. weapons while on tour in Afghanistan remain hazy. (The military first pretended that Tillman died under enemy fire.) A well-read man, Tillman, just before he died, had made an appointment to meet with the antiwar intellectual Noam Chomsky. Tillman was not religious and opposed the Iraq War, and he is rightly considered a national hero. But how would a more anonymous soldier in the military be treated who held similar views about our place in the universe?

Consider the case of Specialist Jeremy Hall, who chose to be honest about his lack of religion. Unlike Tillman, who was used by the military as a propaganda tool, Hall did not have the protection of fame. A superior officer implied to Hall that to get promoted he must put his lack of religion aside and pray with his fellow soldiers. A man of integrity, Hall refused— and didn't receive the promotion. Later, at a meeting of the Military Association of Atheists and Freethinkers organized by Hall, a major crashed the meeting and chastised Hall, threatening disciplinary action.

Because of his personal beliefs, Hall received death threats from fellow soldiers. On leave in Qatar, a group of U.S. soldiers chased Hall, hurling slurs and threatening to beat him. Fearing for Hall's safety, the army assigned him a bodyguard. He eventually chose not to reenlist.

Such harassment is not unique. A 2005 U.S. Air Force report found that officers, faculty, and cadets at the Air Force Academy promoted fundamentalist beliefs and harangued cadets who practiced a different religion or no religion. Media reports have revealed similar incidents in the military, particularly in recent years.

Contrast that with what happens to those officers who actively promote fundamentalist beliefs. In 2006, seven high-ranking uniformed military officials appeared in a video promoting the Christian Embassy, a proselytizing organization led by Bill Bright. Bright founded the multi-million-dollar Campus Crusade for Christ. He signed the 2002 "Land Letter" that offered President George W. Bush religious justifications for invading Iraq. What happened to the uniformed officers in the Christian Embassy video? Two of them, General Robert Caslen and Colonel Lucious Morton, were promoted, despite a reprimand by the Department of Defense's inspector general for their uniformed participation in this evangelical project.

Organizations like the Officers Christian Fellowship (OCF), the Military Ministry of the Campus Crusade for Christ, the Fellowship of Christian Athletes (FCA), and the Christian Military Fellowship (CMF) encourage soldiers to proselytize. The OCF Web site states, "Our purpose is to glorify God by uniting Christian officers for biblical fellowship and outreach, equipping and encouraging them to minister effectively in the military society." They "call on Christian officers to integrate biblical standards of excellence" into their professional responsibilities. They think "local or ship-based chapel activities offer prime venues for Christ-centered outreach and service to a military community. . . . By cooperating with and assisting chaplains and lay leaders, we seek to exalt the Lord Jesus Christ throughout the entire military society."

The OCF operates on almost all of our bases worldwide and counts 15,000 U.S. military personnel as members. This organization seeks to co-opt military resources and personnel to market religious fundamentalism. This active proselytizing leads soldiers like Specialist Hall to seek support from Jason Torpy, a West Point graduate and president of the Military Association of Atheists and Freethinkers.

On bases and ships, chaplains, attached to commanders, work as close advisers on morale, giving them a special status within the chain of command. According to the only federal court decision directly dealing with the military chaplaincy's constitutionality, *Katcoff v. Marsh*, chaplains are to "meet the religious needs of a pluralistic military community." Army chaplains, the court observed, aren't authorized "to proselytize soldiers or their families." Chaplains must not advance one religious viewpoint over another, whether monotheism over other types of theism or theism over nontheism, yet there is no education in religious diversity during the Chaplain Basic Officer Leadership Course.

When my father served in the military, the idea that the military itself would foster religious discrimination or favoritism was unknown. America's military includes a diverse citizenry. That fundamentalism could become embedded as a quasi-official military religion was antithetical to real military values. It still should be.

Religious Bias Hurts Our Health
Women's Health
In 2005, after being raped, a twenty-year-old woman in Tucson, Arizona, made frantic calls to pharmacies trying to fill a prescription for emergency contraception. She finally found a pharmacy carrying the prescription, but was told the pharmacist on duty would not dispense the medication because of the pharmacist's religion. By the time a willing pharmacist was found, the optimal time for taking the medication had passed.

The Guttmacher Institute reports that fundamentalist pharmacists in several states get special permission from state legislatures to ignore their professional duties and to even deny rape victims emergency contraception. Pharmacists have refused to fill prescriptions for contraceptives, including emergency contraceptives, in over fifteen states. Since emergency contraception became available without a prescription for women over the age of seventeen, refusals to provide nonprescription emergency contraception have also been reported.

Pharmacists work in the health-care profession, not in a church. They have the right to consider their own religious beliefs in determining what medical decisions they make for their own care, but their religious bias should never impede fulfillment of their professional duty to patients. The trauma of rape should never be compounded by the denial of access to emergency contraception. Each year, approximately 25,000 women in America become pregnant as a result of rape. Timely access to emergency contraception could help many of these women avoid the additional trauma of an unintended pregnancy.

We must pass the Access to Birth Control Act, which would require prescriptions to be filled without delay; if a pharmacist has a personal objection to filling a legal prescription, the law would require it be filled immediately by another pharmacist. We must also pass the Compassionate Assistance for Rape Emergencies Act, which would mandate that hospitals guarantee rape victims access to emergency contraception, regardless of the religious bias of health-care providers.

Unjust, religiously biased laws pertaining to sexual health have a deep, pervasive, and harmful effect not just in the United States, but also abroad. In 2003 in Ethiopia, Yemmi Samta didn't know that her fourteen-year-old-daughter, Saron, was pregnant until she found Saron unconscious and bleeding profusely on the dirt floor of their hut. Samta begged a neighbor to load Saron onto a donkey cart and take her to the nearest clinic, twelve miles away. The girl died on the journey from blood loss, the result of a back-alley abortion.

In places like Ethiopia, nongovernmental organizations (NGOs) often provide the only option for women and girls who need abortions. Unfortunately, a U.S. policy created under Ronald Reagan often restricts foreign NGOs that receive U.S. family-planning funds from using their own non-U.S. funds to provide clinical abortion services. The NGOs are also often prohibited from advocating for abortion-law reform in their own countries and even from providing accurate medical counseling or referrals regarding abortion.

This global "gag rule" restricts access to basic, accurate women's health information and services. Its existence demonstrates the power of American theocratic forces. These groups view foreign aid funding as a form of leverage, enabling them to impose their religious bias on people in other countries, including many of the most vulnerable and impoverished people on earth.

Since President Reagan initiated the gag rule, women across the globe have been denied health-care services and information they rightfully need and deserve. The global gag rule prohibits a woman from knowing her medical options because to allow her comprehensive information and care would encourage what religious extremists label as immoral actions. Neither Congress nor the president should deny women accurate medical information. To impose a gag rule is to mandate a particular religious bias and to promote religious propaganda based on the views of specially privileged religious groups—and to use tax dollars to do so.

Who sits in the Oval Office determines whether or not the global gag rule stands. Both Presidents Bill Clinton and Barack Obama overturned the policy, while Presidents Reagan, George H. W. Bush, and George W. Bush imposed the gag rule. The lives and rights of women should not hang on one man's edict (or, when we get there, one woman's edict).

Congress must permanently repeal this gag rule, so no matter who's in the Oval Office, federal funds can go to hospitals and clinics that provide comprehensive reproductive information and services, rather than only to those that restrict informing women of all their choices and rights.

Health Education

Policies based on religious bias affect women's health and our children's health and health education. Religious ideology, not medical science, now targets many public school children in health-related curricula across the country. For example, in May 2009, using federal "abstinence-only-until-marriage" funds, the State of Mississippi held a teen abstinence summit. According to the American Civil Liberties Union (ACLU), "The 2009 summit featured religious themes and overtly Christian messages, including a lengthy presentation about the Ten Commandments by Judge John Hudson. Judge Hudson told the audience, 'Abstain, God says, from promiscuous sex. . . . Why would He tell us not to do it? He's not. He's telling us that He created this great and wonderful gift for a special and unique committed relationship that is to last forever.' The program also included several prayers." Yes, that's our tax dollars at work.

Consider what experts say about such programs: the American Academy of Pediatrics states that "abstinence-only programs have not demonstrated successful outcomes with regard to delayed initiation of sexual activity or use of safer sex practices. . . . Programs that offer a discussion of HIV prevention and contraception as the best approach for adolescents who are sexually active have been shown to delay the initiation of sexual activity and increase the proportion of sexually active adolescents who reported using birth control." Similarly, researchers who studied the National Survey of Family Growth to determine the impact of sex education found that teens who received comprehensive sex education were 50 percent less likely to get pregnant than those who received abstinence-only education.

Since 1997 the federal government has allocated more than $1 billion for abstinence-only-until-marriage programs. Making matters worse, by law, abstinence-only-until-marriage programs can't provide lifesaving information about the health benefits of contraception and condoms for the prevention of sexually transmitted infections, including HIV/AIDS and unintended pregnancies. Sex education programs for teens should protect the health and safety of children—not promote a particular religious bias.

Fundamentalists oppose pediatricians, preferring propaganda to information. As the American Academy of Pediatrics recommends, medically accurate sex education programs free from religious bias must be supported. No federal dollars should fund abstinence-only programs. Tax money should go to programs that work, tell the truth about health issues, and respect the separation of church and state.

Life-Saving Health Research

For a worldview that often references God's love, where is the compassion in failing to provide lifesaving information about AIDS? Where is the compassion in prohibiting lifesaving research?

Did you ever know someone who faced leukemia? About a quarter million children and adults in the world develop some form of leukemia every year. Many die. But there's hope. Through embryonic stem cell research, scientists may develop a special type of white blood cell that destroys leukemia cancer cells.

Did you ever know someone who faced diabetes? Millions upon millions face this horrible disease, often resulting in amputation, disability, and death. But, because of embryonic stem cell research, there's hope for the development of cells that produce insulin for the treatment of type 1 diabetes. Stem cell research could prolong the lives of millions of diabetics.

Maybe you know of someone who faced Lou Gehrig's disease or a stroke or Parkinson's disease or a spinal cord injury. Millions of people face these deadly challenges. Embryonic stem cell research offers real hope, but there is a catch. Theocratic extremists object to such basic research. Thousands of embryonic stem cells from fertility clinics across the country are destroyed every year rather than used to advance what the National Institutes of Health says is "one of the most promising areas of research."

Legislation in Congress would allow stem cell research, limiting such research to stem cells from fertility centers that would otherwise be thrown away. And, thankfully, in 2010, the U.S. government authorized trials that could lead to meaningful treatment for spinal cord injury using stem cells that would otherwise be thrown away. But religious extremists want to block even this use of stem cells.

Religious extremists talk about choosing life, yet they halt research that could save millions of lives. Religious extremists say their interpretation of the Bible belongs in our laws, and that human life is less important than their desire to impose their interpretation of the Bible on the rest of us. These religious extremists simply refuse to choose life. We must consistently speak for the health of our fellow human beings born into this world. By speaking out for stem cell research, we are choosing life. Sadly, the fundamentalist theocrats are doing the opposite.

Religious Bias Promotes Discrimination
"Faith-Based" Initiatives
It is unconstitutional to allow religious organizations that get federal funds to hire and fire employees because of their religion. It is unconstitutional to allow religious institutions that get federal money to proselytize to recipients of their government-sponsored social services. It is unconstitutional to send taxpayer dollars to houses of worship. The George W. Bush administration permitted each of these unconstitutional activities, labeling them "faith-based" initiatives. Despite his promise, President Obama has failed to reverse this unconstitutional policy.

President James Madison—Father of the Constitution—vetoed a congressional bill that gave an Episcopal church in the District of Columbia the authority to care for and educate poor children even though the legislation allocated no public funds to the congregation. Madison said it would "be a precedent for giving to religious societies as such a legal agency in carrying into effect a public and civil duty."

The constitutional rights of taxpayers and social service recipients stayed protected from discrimination until President Bush established the White House Office of Faith-Based and Community Initiatives in 2001. The office funneled tax money to religious groups and gave financial advantages to religious institutions over secular nonprofits competing for government funding. Religious institutions have unique advantages in applying for federal money over secular institutions. Houses of worship can get federal funds without first creating a nonprofit 501(c)(3) service organization to separate their sectarian and secular activities. They can also (1) receive grants without segregating the funds from private sources; (2) provide tax-subsidized services in spaces replete with religious symbols; and (3) discriminate in hiring based on religion. This is not an abstract concern. At least one qualified individual was fired from a "faith-based" initiative because he was Muslim. Indeed, Christian fundamentalists have been fired because they are not the right type of fundamentalist.

Jefferson and Madison strictly and vehemently opposed religious discrimination in government-funded entities. To be consistent with our Founders and our Constitution, the U.S. government must overturn all faith-based-initiative executive orders and end preferences for religious organizations. These are the values of our nation's Founders. They must be our values as well. President Obama gave his word in 2008 that he would end proselytizing and discrimination in so-called faith-based initiatives. He has yet to keep his own pledge.

Taxpayer-Funded Religious Propaganda
Voucher programs force every U.S. taxpayer to subsidize private religious schools. These schools discriminate on the basis of religion and proselytize to students who have no choice but to be subjected to propaganda when they should be getting an education. That is an unethical use of your tax money.

In the federally funded Washington, DC, voucher program, more than 80 percent of participating students attend private religious schools. In 2009 in Arizona, more than 50 percent of taxpayer funds donated by the state under a scholarship program went to students who attended religious schools. Our laws protect students in public schools from many forms of discrimination, including religious discrimination. Compare that to the mission statements of these two private schools in Washington, DC, that receive federally funded vouchers:

> *Anacostia Christian Bible School (grades K–6)*: "Our purpose is to turn an audience into an army by reconciling them to God by making warriors for Christ and to each other through worship, prayer, preaching, fellowship, and teaching."

> *Cornerstone Schools of Washington, DC (grades K–6)*: "God's truth is infused throughout the curriculum and is reinforced in chapel each week."

Not only may private religious schools have a religious curriculum, but they may also discriminate against teachers based on religion, ignoring their professional qualifications. Giving tax money to religious institutions without holding them to nondiscrimination law violates our Constitution's central principles.

Since 1967, voters in over twenty states have rejected voucher proposals and other tax-assistance programs for religious schools. American public schools should unify our country's entire range of diverse communities. Vouchers for religious schools undermine this vital unifying function by surrendering the long-standing principle of equal treatment regardless of religion. Your tax money should not fund programs that harm the fundamental civil rights of students, teachers, and other employees.

Boy Scouts of America

Neil Polzin joined the Boy Scouts at age nine. At eighteen Neil earned his Eagle Scout badge. For nine years, Neil worked for the Boy Scouts of America organization as an aquatics director. "Scouts made me who I am," says Neil. "At 14, I became a life guard and began training other life guards—that's how I met my fiancée. . . . The rescue skills that Scouts taught me enabled me to save lives; on a hiking trip I came across a stranded hiker and my Scouts survival skills allowed me to climb down a ravine and perform first-aid for seven hours until the hiker could be rescued by an emergency helicopter."

Yet, after almost two decades and top commendations, Neil was ordered to "sever any ties" with the Boy Scouts of America in June 2009. The Boy Scouts "did not feel he was a capable role model for children." Why? Because he doesn't have a belief in god. Not only did the Boy Scouts fire Neil, the organization also told him to never again contact anyone from his troop.

Neil's story is no isolated incident. Many American families are hurt by the Boy Scouts' discriminatory practices that bar both children and adults without a "god belief" from participation. This discrimination continues with your tax dollars.

In 2005 Congress passed a resolution encouraging the Department of Defense to support Boy Scout activities through the use of military personnel, federal land, and other assistance for its massive jamborees. The 2005 jamboree alone cost taxpayers approximately $8 million. Then, in 2006, Congress included the Support Our Scouts Act in its defense authorization bill. This law requires the Department of Defense to provide at least the same level of support for the Boy Scout's national and world jamborees as in past years. This law also requires any state or local government entity that receives Community Development Block Grant money from the Department of Housing and Urban Development to allow the Boy Scouts to have meetings in its facilities or on its property. This requirement overrides local antidiscrimination laws forbidding access to a discriminatory group.

In 2008 Congress directed the U.S. Mint to produce commemorative Boy Scouts coins as a $3.5 million fundraiser for the Boy Scouts of America. Federal funding of the Boy Scouts allows the organization to continue discriminating against those without a belief in god and to teach young boys that only believers in god can be "good citizens." Many boys with a naturalistic worldview violate their own consciences to remain scouts.

The "Declaration of Religious Principle" found in the Boy Scout's bylaws must be affirmed by every participant, volunteer, and employee. This declaration states that "no member can grow into the best kind of citizen without recognizing an obligation to God. . . . The recognition of God as the ruling and leading power in the universe and the grateful acknowledgment of His favors and blessings are necessary to the best type of citizenship and are wholesome precepts in the education of the growing members." Apparently the Boy Scouts believe that many Girl Scouts are not "the best kind of citizen" since the Girl Scouts, unlike the Boy Scouts, do not discriminate based on sexual orientation nor on the basis of religion.

To the Boy Scouts of America, Warren Buffett is a deficient citizen. Using tax dollars to impose religious bias on others is immoral and unconstitutional. The Boy Scouts of America also continues its taxpayer-funded tradition of discrimination against gay people. This tiresome hostility to gay people is an absolute passion in some religious circles. If you want to discriminate against gay people in your church or in your services, that's up to you. Mean as it is, you have a constitutional right to enshrine prejudice in your church and structure marriages—within your church—as you see fit. However, religious prejudice should not be imposed on civil law.

Civil Marriage

More than fifty-five years after they fell in love, eighty-four-year-old Phyllis Lyon and eighty-seven-year-old Del Martin became the first same-sex couple to legally exchange marriage vows in California on June 16, 2008. But the U.S. government's Defense of Marriage Act prohibited recognition of their marriage by any other states or by the federal government. They can't get any of the more than 1,100 federal protections and responsibilities—including social security and immigration benefits—that apply to married couples.

Civil marriage involves a state license. The state conveys no religious blessing with this license. Some people have a religious ceremony, but the ceremony has no legal standing. The civil marriage contract should not require adherence to any specific religious doctrine.

Civil-marriage law was historically used to legally encode segregation. Blacks and whites couldn't marry each other in some states until the Supreme Court overturned "miscegenation" laws in 1967. There were biblical justifications for this form of marriage discrimination as well.

Theological definitions for civil contracts must be opposed and the repeal of the Defense of Marriage Act must be supported. Constitutional amendments seeking to define marriage as "one man, one woman" must also be opposed.

Religious bias is the primary justification for injustice against gay citizens. This bias is repugnant in law.

Religious Bias Harms Our Communities

The County of Boulder in Colorado has employed careful land-use planning designed to balance the needs of its citizens and the need to preserve open space. Its land-use law passed in a local democratic process. Everyone must obey the law—except a megachurch that sought a sixth expansion of its facility and successfully challenged the law in court.

Why was this megachurch successful in its suit? The federal Religious Land Use and Institutionalized Persons Act (RLUIPA) privileges religion by providing a broad exemption to the enforcement of any land-use regulations when, and only when, such regulations are challenged by a religious organization. RLUIPA is labeled as protecting religious freedom, but its title is misleading. The free expression clause of the First Amendment continues to protect religious freedom as always. Congressional action to "restore" a freedom, such as the ability to ignore laws others must obey, is nothing more than special rights dressed up pretty.

The rest of us can't ignore zoning laws with an artificially created loophole. For those who believe in local control, consider that local elected representatives in Boulder County made a decision meant to benefit the community as a whole. Yet, because of a top-down federal mandate, religions are exempted from local law. These top-down federal mandates riddle our legal code with exemptions for specific religious sects, leaving other religious groups and the nonreligious in a state of second-class citizenship.

A nonprofit that serves the poor must obey the law. Why then should a megachurch that focuses on preaching against gay people be exempt from zoning law? A for-profit software company must obey zoning laws. Why then should a megachurch that preaches that women should be subservient be able to expand its buildings willy-nilly ignoring local law? Who does more for society? The software developer? Or the megachurch? The nonprofit that helps poor people? Or the megachurch?

These laws also impose federal authority on purely local issues. Talk about top-down. The federal government comes in and picks who must (or need not) obey local laws. Our abiding American value, equal treatment under the law, calls out for repeal of this unjust special right in law.

Religious Bias Degrades Our Schools

Hundreds of thousands of public school children are misled by taxpayer-funded religious propaganda in multiple ways. In 2009, the Texas Board of Education voted to present "all sides" when studying evolution and misleadingly required consideration of "gaps" in the fossil record. Stated former Texas Board of Education member Don McLeroy, "Evolution is hooey." That year it also voted to remove from curriculum standards reference to the strong scientific consensus that the universe began more than 13 billion years ago.

In March 2010 the Texas Board of Education voted to remove Thomas Jefferson's name from a list of leaders who have inspired changes in governments worldwide. Why? It might have something to do with the fact that President Jefferson, who authored the Declaration of Independence, also penned the phrase "separation of church and state."

Although this reference to Jefferson was later reinstated, students taking government classes in Texas get told that America's founding was informed by the Judeo-Christian legal tradition and "especially Biblical law" and that the legal principles of "Moses . . . informed the American founding documents." In fact, as Steven K. Green, director of the Center for Religion, Law and Democracy at Willamette University, states, the Founders "did not draw on Mosaic law." Indeed, the Enlightenment developed in opposition to reliance on biblical law, and our nation's founders were strong proponents of the Enlightenment. Green's research of late-1700s American court cases that referenced Mosaic law yielded almost nothing: "The record is basically bereft."

Texas's influence reaches well beyond the state line. Because other big states (e.g., California and New York) don't impose statewide standards in the same way, Texas remains one of the largest statewide textbook markets. The Texas government buys or distributes a staggering 48 million textbooks annually, which strongly inclines educational publishers to tailor products to fit Texas standards. Even if this problem were limited only to Texas, we wouldn't be content to leave approximately 4.8 million Texas public school children behind. It's unacceptable for any child to be subjected to religious propaganda in a taxpayer-funded school.

The Obama administration has embraced common core educational standards developed by the National Governors Association. Although the administration offers financial incentives for states to adopt similar standards, these standards apply only to math and language arts. George Will, the conservative columnist, views science and history as "neglected" in national standards. If there are to be national standards at all, government must give to science and history the same weight it gives to language arts and math, with no pandering to religious bias.

Presidents John F. Kennedy and Dwight D. Eisenhower strongly supported federal efforts to improve science education. Their positions were uncontroversial at the time. President Kennedy said, "Science contributes to our culture in many ways, as a creative intellectual activity in its own right, as the light which has served to illuminate man's place in the universe, and as the source of understanding of man's own nature." But the *New York Times* noted in March 2010 that some basic, factual subjects, such as evolution, may be deemed "controversial" in the twenty-first-century educational environment. Whether we will teach our students the truth about science and history has now become a point of political contention, as religious bias competes with reality.

A few theocratic Texans shouldn't get to determine the educational standards for America's schools. We must therefore press for educational standards equity as essential for America's future. Just as national standards for math and language arts have been developed and embraced by the Obama administration, the National Governors Association, and many members of Congress, so should common core standards for science and history be given equal weight. Textbooks and teachers must present accurate information on evolution, the age of the universe, America's secular founding, and laws affecting church-state separation.

Religious Bias Robs Us of Our Dignity

Religious bias is the primary argument against death-with-dignity laws, affecting the liberty of those seniors and terminally ill facing difficult end-of-life decisions. Oregon has successfully administered such a law since 1994. Washington passed a similar law in 2008. The term physician-assisted suicide is misleading. In the circumstances specified by these northwestern statutes, a person, already diagnosed with a terminal illness, is permitted to choose an alternative manner of death. Death is a foregone conclusion, out of the patient's control. The individual seeks only to make his or her own decision about how he or she dies. Religious bias is the primary motivation for this restriction on an individual's decision regarding his or her own body. Compassion and reason mandate that individual choice be honored. A federal law must be passed supporting this individual liberty. Until then, no federal law should restrict those states that have secured such a statutory right for their residents. Similarly, religious hospitals should honor do-not-resuscitate orders and other advance directives from patients—or the hospital should forgo federal funds.

Religious Bias Hurts Our Children
Child-Care Centers
Deaths in religious child-care centers, as discussed in this book's introductory chapter, are rare but emblematic of a pervasive injustice. They are horrific examples of the many harmful consequences of America's continuing shift toward theocracy, particularly over the last four decades. A more in-depth understanding of how religious child-care exemptions in law can be abused illustrates the broader problem we face as a society when it comes to the crumbling wall separating church and state.

Child-care standards represent minimum standards designed for the best interests of children. It's wrong that one set of child-care providers should be subject to rules and regulations, while another category of child-care business gets special rights to ignore the very same laws. The National Association of Child Care Resource and Referral Agencies says, "When states categorically exempt centers sponsored by churches . . . children are less protected and the whole regulation system is weakened."

In Alabama, where at least two children have died in religious child-care centers, one fly-by-night religious child-care provider that had lost its lease stayed in business by moving around, switching children from apartment to apartment. Who looked out for the children in this tawdry, vagabond business as it bounced from location to location? The state sure wasn't helping. Since religious child-care centers remain exempt from state inspection, the state didn't know for some time that the religious child-care provider had no fixed location. Bad things can, and do, happen at secular child-care centers, but the lack of inspection and the lack of any health and safety laws inevitably leads to greater risks for children in Alabama's religious child-care centers as a whole. Even if one takes the libertarian perspective that there should be no regulation at all, surely no one can justify two entirely separate laws for like facilities, the only difference being religion.

In one religious child-care center, investigators found children sitting in feces-filled diapers for nearly four hours. In another religious child-care center, children were forced to use outdoor porta-johns instead of functioning toilets. In another religious child-care center, where dirty carpets were littered with dirty diapers, one adult "tended" to nine babies—in a building with no fire sprinkler!

The religious exemption also serves as a refuge for scofflaws. For example, the owner of three nonreligious child-care centers was ordered to suspend the transportation portion of one of his facilities after a driver at one of them allegedly left a child unattended in a van. Rather than comply, this owner, shall we say, "got religion," and filed his religious license exemption—solely for that one facility. Despite the documented suspension, the "religious" child-care paperwork sailed through and the owner continued to ignore the transportation-safety regulations for children—all under the transparent pretext of being a religious facility.

In the past, owners of religious child-care centers in Alabama at least had to file an affidavit stating that their centers were in compliance with health and safety laws. Even this minimal requirement is no more, because one Alabama governor removed the affidavit requirement for religious child-care centers. Yet still, your federal tax money flows to these religious child-care centers, which can ignore the law that secular child-care centers must follow.

Several states in addition to Alabama give special rights to religious child-care centers. When the Florida government shut down Lillie Laster Jones's secular child-care center because of repeated violations of health and safety regulations, Jones knew just what to do: set up a religious child-care center so the law could be ignored. Less than one week after being forced to shut down her secular child-care center—where a toddler was found wandering a deserted playground in only a diaper—Jones opened up her new "religious" child-care center. By affiliating with a church, Jones could operate beyond the scrutiny of state child-welfare officials through a religious exemption to Florida's child-care laws. Only the church and the religious accrediting entity approved by the state could monitor the health, safety, and sanitation of her child-care center.

Two years later, Jones's "religious" child-care center was shut down when a fourteen-year-old sexually assaulted a five-year-old under Jones's supervision. Jones's response? Six days later, she reopened her religious child-care center under a new name in a new location upon receiving approval by a religious "accreditation" agency. Consider this: religious child-care centers in Florida like Lillie Laster Jones's can get federal funding as long as they are associated with a church or parochial school and are endorsed by a private, religious accrediting agency.

More than ten states allow federally funded, unlicensed religious child-care facilities. Depending on the state, this can mean that some of these religious child-care facilities are exempt from a broad range of health and safety laws. Others are offered fewer exemptions, but the real question is why would any exemption exist at all, particularly when the safety of children is at stake?

Child-care centers are businesses, but they are not your neighborhood convenience story. These businesses are charged with caring for our communities' youngest and most innocent—one of the most important tasks in which society engages. This type of business can have significant and long-lasting impacts, for better or worse, not only on individual children but also on the health of our communities and our economy. The United States invests billions in federal funds on child care each year, including through Child Care Development Block Grants, Temporary Assistance for Needy Families (TANF), Head Start, and more.

In the late 1980s, America nearly passed federal child-care standards. Child advocates, educators, and parents were united in support. But religious child-care centers wanted your federal tax dollars, without having to conform to federal standards. So religious groups went to President George H. W. Bush and got just what they wanted—they killed the standards and continued to get the money.

So know this: in Alabama about 25 percent of children in "religious" child-care centers receive federal tax dollars through child-care subsidies.

Federal money benefiting state child care should be contingent on uniform child-care health and safety laws. Your tax money should not be grabbed by those who ignore basic health and safety laws for children just because they label themselves religious.

Such abuses extend beyond religious child-care centers, because exemptions are often made at the primary- and secondary-school level as well. For example, in the 1990s, the Rolf "disciplinary" school in Texas was cited for whipping sixteen teen girls and placing them in solitary confinement. Despite numerous such incidents, then governor George W. Bush sought a statute exempting religious businesses like the Rolf school from many safety standards. Later, after Bush's exemption passed, the Rolf school was convicted of criminal conduct for requiring boys to dig a filthy pit while being subjected to sleep deprivation. You know a policy has gone too far when even the Texas legislature feels compelled to withdraw an exemption championed by Bush. Yet, some other states, including Missouri, continue to allow such schools to function.

Legislatures across the United States that exempt religious child-care centers by law made a moral choice. Or was it an immoral choice?

Children's Medical "Care"

I served in Maine's legislature ten years, including a term in legislative leadership. Maine is not a state dominated by fundamentalists. And yet, in Maine, parents can deny their infant eyedrops—eyedrops that prevent blindness—if the parents simply state that they wish to deny their child medical care for religious reasons.

It doesn't end there. If parents simply say they are religious, then Maine exempts them from having their children tested for lead levels. If parents simply say they're religious, then Maine exempts their children from receiving vaccines for measles, mumps, and diphtheria. Religious vaccine exemptions exist in the vast majority of states despite the fact that the person deciding is not the child who may become severely ill or die. Furthermore, such exemptions endanger children who come in contact with unvaccinated children.

Thousands of adults treat their children as religious property based on the Epistle of James and other ancient texts. Christian Science "nurses" are completely untrained, but they themselves have reported trying to "heal" children who were convulsing violently, vomiting repeatedly, urinating uncontrollably. How—and why—these "nurses" could watch such torture, and not rush them to a hospital, is morally astounding.

Federal law exempts so-called faith healing from the minimum federal definition of medical neglect under the Child Abuse and Prevention Treatment Act (CAPTA). I'd be completely for so-called faith healing if there were actual healing involved. That's the problem: there is no healing. Let's call it what it is: faith harming or, in the worst cases, faith killing. Next time you hear someone use the term faith healing, please let them know of the real torture involved. Leaving aside the horrific deaths, think of the many more children who have been "merely" tortured and disabled due to faith harming. This is particularly hideous in those cases when the pain is preventable and the illness is curable through modern medicine.

In the book *When Prayer Fails*, Shawn Francis Peters details the horrors resulting from so-called faith healing:

- A two-year-old is left to bleed to death from an easily treatable cut.

- A tumor grows from a four-year-old's eye, equaling the size of the child's head. As the child walks through her home blood trails are left on the walls as her massive tumor smears the house. Later the child dies.

- A child's untreated tumor results in the amputation of a limb, because the parent believes that the child was being punished for sin that could only be cured through prayer.

- A two-year-old with a treatable bowel obstruction dies after vomiting fecal matter. The two-year-old screamed in agony for several horrific days before dying.

- A twelve-year-old's treatable tumor is allowed to grow to over three feet in diameter. When the child is finally hospitalized, the staff and patients are overwhelmed with the smell of decaying flesh that permeated the entire floor of the hospital. Later the child dies.

- An eight-year-old girl is left in "excruciating pain" for two weeks from treatable meningitis before she eventually dies.

A study by the National Center for Child Abuse and Neglect states that "more children are actually being abused in the name of God than in the name of Satan." We don't know how many children are killed each year by "faith healing." Some deaths are entirely uninvestigated and not included in statistics. However, a study of Faith Assembly congregations, many of whom use "faith healing," found that the mortality rate for Faith Assembly infants in their first four weeks was 270 percent higher than the national average.

I know you might be thinking, Tennessee (Jessica Crank), Alabama (Amiyah White), just stay away from the Bible Belt, and you're fine. In fact, largely due to the stamp of approval for such exemptions at the federal level, over thirty-five states offer some form of faith-harming exemptions from commonsense child protection laws that the rest of us must obey.

The largest outbreak of measles in the last two decades in the United States occurred in Missouri. Why? The measles took hold in a number of Christian Science schools and spread from there. The result? The state had a handful of entirely preventable deaths and witnessed the needless suffering of numerous children. On top of this, public school children experienced countless hours of lost school time and missed valuable educational instruction, while families lost wages due to parents having to stay home with their sick kids, leading to the waste of taxpayer money.

Bizarre sects outside the Bible Belt include a sect in Massachusetts with secretive rituals and "faith-healing" practices that buried small children in a "holy ceremony" at Mt. Katahdin in Maine. Christian Scientists are more well known than this sect, but both contribute not to freedom but to isolation and endangerment of children.

The Constitution prohibits religious discrimination, so any religion, no matter how small, can claim "faith-healing" protection. Once a government gives its stamp of approval to religious child abuse to one denomination or sect, the government is constitutionally bound to accept this same behavior from all denominations—and judgments as to which religion is bizarre or fly-by-night is not relevant. Consider one so-called Internet-based Native American "religion" whose leader happens not to be Native American. One boy's parent, also non-Native American, claimed adherence to this new-found religion and refused to have him treated for a treatable cancer.

So, where are the self-proclaimed "right-to-life" groups when it comes to Amiyah White dying alone in that van? Life is sacred, they say. Where were they for fifteen-year-old Jessica Crank?

More importantly, where were we? Why aren't all of us who care about basic human rights organizing and calling Congress right now? Federal law should have one standard for protecting children from abuse and neglect—not one standard that applies to most of us but that allows a chosen few to intentionally ignore the desperate medical needs of their children, all in the name of religion.

It is not enough to simply eliminate the various exemptions at both the federal and state level. Federal and state statutes should impose civil liabilities on "faith-healing" treatment providers. In addition, federal dollars for state child-abuse programs must be made contingent on a uniform child-medical-neglect standard.

Politicians sometimes justify these horrific legal exemptions as a religious constitutional right. This is a lie. The Supreme Court ruled in 1943 in *Prince v. Massachusetts* that the religious have no constitutional right "to make martyrs of their children." Medical science and compassion must be the decisive factors in children's health.

Today, the exemptions in federal and state law are the result of lobbying that places religious special rights above basic ethics, a basic sense of humanity, and basic science. The American Medical Association, the American Academy of Pediatrics, and the National District Attorney's Association all oppose religious exemptions for so-called faith healing. Doing away with the torture of children is a moral imperative.

As with the exemptions given to religious child-care centers, legislatures across the United States that exempt "faith healing" from child-abuse and child-neglect laws made a moral choice. Or was it an immoral choice?

Sexual Abuse
Religious exemptions in child care, and religious child-sacrifice exemptions,

are less notorious than a third form of child abuse: pedophilia. Sexual abuse certainly isn't a problem unique to priests. I knew excellent priests at the University of Notre Dame, during my studies in Ireland, and when I served with the Jesuit Volunteer Corps in a Yupik town in Alaska. So I don't paint all priests with one brush, and it's a sad reality that pedophilia extends well beyond the walls of the Catholic Church. But how has the Church handled charges of abuse? It is the institutional decisions that are most reprehensible and utterly immoral.

The reason? Let me explain by example.

Bishop Thomas Daily knew—knew!—from more than one report that a priest in his jurisdiction had made more than one positive statement about man-boy sex. Indeed, Bishop Daily had reason to believe that the priest had attended Man-Boy Love Association meetings.

Forget priests. What should and would any sensible and moral employer do under such circumstances? Well, as someone who started a children's museum back in Maine, let me suggest two obvious reactions: first, remove the suspect from any position that involves access to minors until an investigation is conducted, and second, request an investigation by proper law enforcement authorities. What did Bishop Daily do in response? Isolate the priest? Report the matter to the police? No. He gave the priest a promotion. I repeat. He gave the priest a promotion and transferred him from one parish to the next, thus endangering even more children.

It gets worse. In a 1993 piece written for the *Boston Globe*, Father Andrew Greeley calculated that there were 100,000 victims of pedophile priests in the United States. This estimate comes from a respected priest—before the worst of the charges about pedophile priests surfaced. Whatever the actual number, let's focus on two things: (1) the systemic pervasiveness of the problem and (2) the legal defense that the Church has asserted. Church lawyers argued that internal administrative documents and decisions (like moving suspected pedophiles from parish to parish) was, get this, religious free expression. Walk through this looking glass again: Church lawyers argue that covering up employment policies regarding pedophiles is a form of religious free expression. Church leadership successfully delayed cases with this argument.

Physical Abuse

The specifically religious justifications for legal exemptions that put children at greater physical risk are not isolated but part of a pattern. Consider this interesting quote: "Pain is a marvelous purifier." These are not the words of an avowed masochist, or a sadist. These are the words of

James Dobson, easily one of the most powerful religious leaders in America today, author of books such as *Dare to Discipline*. Dobson's organization, Focus on the Family, has an annual budget of over $100 million.

Let's be clear: when James Dobson says "pain is a marvelous purifier," he means pain for children. Dobson asserts, "spanking should be of sufficient magnitude to cause the child to cry genuinely." Dobson advocates spanking children as young as eighteen months.

Dobson states that if children cry for more than five minutes, "the child is merely complaining" and "I would require him to stop the protest crying, usually by offering him a little more of whatever caused the original tears." As a former assistant attorney general who handled numerous child-protection cases, I assure you that such a practice could easily result in tragedy. Given the sway of Mr. Dobson, I fear for the children who attend one of the religious schools that has the "privilege" of using corporal punishment (not to mention the many children in homes under the influence of Dobson's "moral" pronouncements). Unfortunately Dobson's disturbing attitude is not an isolated one.

Michael Pearl—another prominent fundamentalist and author whose books have sold over 1.8 million copies—influences parents and teachers in fundamentalist schools nationwide. Regarding child discipline, Pearl states, "A length of quarter-inch plumbing supply line is a real attention-getter." It certainly got some attention when a seven-year-old girl died after an apparent repeated beating—with a "quarter-inch plumbing supply line." A parent had listened carefully to Mr. Pearl's detailed suggestion.

The Bible does contain several passages that specifically recommend inflicting pain on children as a method of discipline. (For that matter, the Bible contains statements condoning things like stonings and slavery.) Of course, most Christians don't support corporal punishment. Yet Mr. Dobson and Mr. Pearl remain prominent leaders in a widespread movement and, according to at least one study, 66 percent of fundamentalist Protestants believe corporal punishment should be allowed in public schools.

Most states prohibit corporal punishment in public schools. Less than five states prohibit corporal punishment in private schools. Well over a million children go to private fundamentalist schools, schools that are more likely to authorize corporal punishment today than other types of schools. A high percentage of Christian schools remain exempt from laws prohibiting corporal punishment while millions in tax dollars make their way into their coffers. In this way the United States government authorizes the use of physical violence as a form of punishment for a specific set of children.

Children in religious schools are no less human—and no less deserving of safety from physical harm—than other children. Laws against corporal punishment in schools must apply equally to both public and private schools. In short, striking kids to enforce discipline should be prohibited in all public and private schools that receive federal dollars. American law must be consistent, especially when it involves our children and our tax money.

No ancient document should be called on to authorize harm to another human being, simply because it's an ancient or an allegedly supernatural document. Why should religious bias justify placing children in distinct situations of danger?

* * * * *

In this chapter we have seen religious bias harm children, harm public health, harm our men and women in uniform, harm our seniors, harm our citizenry, and harm our schools—all at taxpayers expense. This is not the American way. America is still the greatest nation on earth because of its commitment to equal treatment under the law, its protection of minority rights, and its separation of church and state under the Constitution. The injustices described in this chapter corrode these most sacred American ideals. Deeply connected to this corrosive trend in American life is the pervasive and widespread desire among religious extremists to control the most intimate aspects of other people's lives.

4 Genital Morality vs. Real Morality

Marriage has historically never meant anything other than a man and a woman. It has never meant two men, two women, a man and his pet, or a man and a whole herd of pets.

—Mike Huckabee

The big thing is to make this country . . . quit discriminating against people just because they're gay.

—Barry Goldwater

I quit watching broadcast TV shortly after *Seinfeld* closed up shop. The way I see it, most TV shows just aren't that good, and, when TV is available, the strong temptation exists to watch stuff—just because stuff's there.

Let's pick an example: *Dynasty* was one of the top-rated shows of the 1980s. Watch it again and you find it's kind of boring. *Dynasty* is more representative of TV in general than are the quality shows. Yet, those few nuggets do exist. Take, for example, the original *Star Trek* (yep, I'm a nerd), which captures Kennedy-era idealism well—that desire to boldly go where no man has gone before. Shakespeare it's not, but *Star Trek* is iconic TV that resonates today. As another example, take *Twilight Zone*, which offers Kennedy-era morality plays—classic "what you can do for your country" ideals wearing the mask of sci-fi and hocus-pocus good fun.

Star Trek and *Twilight Zone* were produced in the 1960s, but let's consider (and I'm sneaking up on sex here) another show set in the 1960s, a show that raises the immortal question: what would Don Draper do? Well, he does a lot of alcohol—and cigarettes for that matter—and there was that episode with the stewardess.

The Don Draper character is expressly Republican and not someone whose values I personally admire overall. That said, he is a Republican of a libertarian (some would say libertine) bent. Republicans today say they're

65

libertarians . . . all while they try to regulate your bedroom for Jesus. (I'll beat up a bit on liberals later.)

As a lobbyist and advocate for secularism in the halls of Congress, I am familiar with the many religiously motivated policies that focus on sex. The previous chapter touched on three examples: (1) abstinence-only sex education, which often peddles biblical subservience to women and leads to higher rates of HIV and unplanned pregnancies; (2) laws that allow fundamentalist pharmacists to violate their professional responsibility and refuse to fill prescriptions; and (3) the "gag rule," which prevents women around the world from receiving health-care services and accurate information they rightfully need and deserve. But the list of biblically justified sexual and sexist suppression goes on.

A fourth example: You may know about Title IX because of its relevance to equity in school sports for young women. However, a less well-known aspect of the law is the requirement that girls and young women be treated equitably not just in sports but in education overall. It's less well known because, even in 1972, when the law was enacted, equity in academics was less controversial than equity in sports. However, a little-known provision in Title IX states that religious schools can treat males and females unequally—if it is a tenet of their religion. That's right, if, and only if, sexism is a religious tenet, then the United States government is willing to permit it. Why should even one child be taught that women should be subservient? Children make no adult choice to attend a sexist school. It violates their human rights to impose such views on them.

A fifth example: Although the horrific term "female genital mutilation" calls to mind girls in Middle Eastern and North African lands, numerous American girls have been transported out of the United States to be subjected to this hideous procedure. Our laws and policies must do more to protect these vulnerable girls.

A sixth example: Fundamentalists notoriously call for separate and unequal treatment for gay people, particularly those straight-as-an-arrow male fundamentalist preacher types—like George Rekers, the guy who "treats" gay men to "cure" them of their gayness. Oh, wait. That's right. My mistake. Rekers is the minister who was caught with his "rent boy" at the airport in Miami. To be fair, maybe he's the rare exception—just look at that other theocratic preacher against gay sex, Ted Haggard. Oh, that's right . . . well, never mind, you get the idea. Some of these fundamentalist ministers must only be homophobic, not brazen hypocrites, too.

Nosy-minded busybodies like Rekers and Haggard call to mind an old saying we have back in Maine. You may have heard it: mind your own business! Whatever happened to this bit of reasonable common sense? Gossips and Peeping Toms, whether secular or religious, are some of the most disgusting slimeballs you can possibly meet, but gossipy sex lecturers are particularly noxious when they can poke around in other people's sex lives with the imprimatur of law. Why? Three reasons.

First, someone is hurt. There is a real human victim—often women, sometimes sexual minorities—when religious sexual meddling imposes its mean-spirited will on American law.

Second, these laws are justified by pointing to an ancient text. Take a step back and think on it for a moment. Assume that I proposed to take away another citizen's human rights, and that I justified taking away those rights by referring to, let's say, an ancient, one-thousand-year-old parchment from, say, Romania. You'd say that's an absolutely wacko justification for denying human rights. However, if I change the hypothetical to a two-thousand-year-old document from the Levant and, if I further assert that this two-thousand-year-old document has supernatural powers, then the politicians fall over themselves bowing low and deep in subservience. How utterly medieval—yet widely accepted in the twenty-first century.

Third, all of these religiously biased regulations against women and various forms of sexuality come down to the premise that "privileged males rule"—perhaps because that's who wrote the rules back in the Bronze Age, when guys could simply hit or rape any women who dared to talk back. Don't believe that was the case? The Bible tells us such acts are A-OK.

The fact that "privileged guys rule" has been dressed up for such a long time as "holy" is something of a testament to the defining power of religious culture and attitudes. Human sexuality and Bronze Age attitudes about human sexuality are perhaps the central characteristic of fundamentalist and theocratic public policy.

The credence that's given to these attitudes results largely from the perceived august authority that religion bestows on them. Indeed, one must stand in awe when one considers the cultural power and pervasiveness of religious law that stands to this day.

The roots of such attitudes run deep—and strange. We all know many religions teach sodomy is a sin, right? Yet, here's a little something about sodomy you may not know: "sodomy," as originally defined by the Catholic Church in its heyday (as a Notre Dame graduate, where else would I look to for such information?), included heterosexual intercourse with the woman on top. In fact, this form of sodomy was so sinful that the priest alone could not forgive you. If the woman was on top, this required seeking forgiveness from the bishop. Can you picture this conversation with a priest? "Forgive me, Father, for I have sinned, er, specifically, I . . ." "Sorry," says the priest, "That's way above my pay grade. You'll have to take that one to the bishop."

The message? Never let a woman get on top. Keep her down, literally and figuratively. Need more examples? How about Deuteronomy 22:13–21, which says that a woman who is not a virgin bride must be killed. What is with religion's obsession with this virgin business anyway?

And then there's Deuteronomy 25:11–12, which says that a married woman must have her hand cut off for touching another guy's penis, even if nonsexually. This seems to take matters a bit far.

OK, so women get stoning and severed hands. But what about the rules for the guys? Well, Genesis 25:1–6 expressly allows mistresses and concubines for guys. (Sorry, ladies, but scripture is scripture.)

What about the New Testament? First Corinthians 14:34–35 requires that women keep silent and learn from husbands, and First Timothy 2:11–13 tells women to "learn in silence with all subjugation."

But, heck, aren't we the America of "independence"—of Wild West–style freedom? Those old biblical rules don't apply to us, right?

Genital Morality: The Bedroom Police

America does indeed have some Wild West traditions. For instance, in the late 1800s, our Supreme Court ruled that a corporation is a person. In that era they held that these so-called persons had "rights." These so-called corporate rights included paying slave wages to little children to work in mines. Children lost their fingers in the cotton mills. That was freedom for corporate America in the late 1800s.

Think of it. No laws, federal or state, when it came to protecting children in the workplace. Lots of "freedom," if you want to call it that, regarding how to exploit poor children in a mine.

Yet in the same era, the government enacted a federal statute—known as the Comstock Act—that made it illegal to deliver or transport "obscene, lewd, or lascivious material." References to birth control met the obscenity definition of this statute. The man who championed the law to Congress, crusader Anthony Comstock, was one of the most powerful people of whom most Americans have never heard. Comstock just so happened to become the enforcer of the very law he had successfully spearheaded (convenient, no?).

Defining obscenity is ridiculously arbitrary business, so what types of material, aside from information on birth control, did Comstock deem "obscene"? Well, Comstock called George Bernard Shaw—the only person to win both an Academy Award and a Nobel Prize for Literature—"an Irish smut peddler." Shaw had written a play about a smart woman who ran a brothel. An early supporter of women's rights, Shaw was a nonreligious human-rights activist who said, "All great truths begin as blasphemies."

Comstock made sure Walt Whitman was fired from his government job because Whitman wrote *Leaves of Grass*, which called on the reader to "re-examine all you have been told at school or church or in any book, dismiss whatever insults your own soul, and your very flesh shall be a great poem." Comstock also got Victoria Woodhull, the first-ever female candidate for U.S. president, imprisoned. Candidate Woodhull advocated free love, women's rights, lenient divorce, and birth control. You can understand why Comstock threw her in the slammer.

It is written that Anthony Comstock destroyed 15 tons of books, 284,000 pounds of plates that would have printed books he did not like, and nearly 4,000,000 pictures. Comstock boasted that he was responsible for 4,000 arrests and 15 suicides. One woman, an advocate for women's rights and birth control, wrote specifically in her suicide note that it was continual harassment by Comstock that sent her over the edge.

Comstock also had Emma Goldman, a very early advocate of gay rights and a prominent voice for free love, jailed twice for distribution of birth control information. Once Goldman stayed in jail for two weeks rather than pay a fine that she actually could afford to pay. She stayed so that she might meet more of the people in prison and learn from their experiences. Goldman was a bit radical for my blood, but I love her. She called Comstock the leader of the "moral eunuchs" and famously said, "If there won't be dancing at the revolution, I'm not coming."

Real Sexual Morality: The Principle of Consent and the Nature of Sex

I suggest that we should indeed have a strong sense of sexual morality, but not the sexual morality of what Emma Goldman called the "moral eunuchs." As a former assistant attorney general who in my brief time oversaw scores of child-protection cases, and as a ten-year legislator who chaired a sex-crime commission, I suggest that sexual morality can be captured in two words: consenting adults. The word "consent" excludes an inappropriate power imbalance—or it is not true consent. The word "adults," meanwhile, excludes priests having sex with boys and preachers having sex with teenage girls. Perhaps most importantly, this principle puts men and women on equal footing, unlike the Victorian and Bronze Age morality of men like Comstock.

Thankfully, bold voices, like those of Goldman, eventually started to tear away at biblical "morality" and increase freedoms for women. Economics have changed things for women, too. So has science—and Mexican yams, the prime ingredient of "the Pill."

The Pill was first marketed in 1960, and by 1969 more than half of college coeds had used it. Through the science of studying sexuality and reproduction, women's sexual options have grown much broader—and they may grow broader and more autonomous still.

Consider a recent study by Meredith Chivers. This is the type of study that could be upsetting to fundamentalists. It basically involved showing a lot of different kinds of porn to people of different sexual orientations, but its results illustrate an interesting point about the nature of our sexuality.

The results? Straight guys tend to be aroused primarily by erotic images of women. Gay men tend to be aroused primarily by erotic images of men. No shocks so far. Lesbians are a bit more variable, but, in general, they tend to be aroused primarily by erotic images of other women. However, self-identified straight women tend to get aroused by, well, a lot of things. Erotic images of men, sure, and, yes, images of gay male erotica. Counterintuitively, self-identified straight women tended to get most turned on by erotic images of women.

The results of this study reflect perhaps not so much a change in women's sexuality as, maybe, the beginnings of a new era in which women (heretofore restricted by patriarchy) will be free to, as the old song goes, "act naturally." Women should not be required by anyone anywhere to do anything in bed, certainly not at the command of men. Neither should they be prohibited from doing whatever they choose with a consenting adult.

But acting naturally is not so naturally accepted by the likes of Anthony Comstock, nor is it acceptable to his modern-day counterparts—men like David Vitter, Mark Sanford, and John Ensign. You know the type. Our sexual overlords.

Just as we should be open-minded about female sexuality, let's take a fresh look at male sexuality as well.

Let us begin with the "million-dollar challenge." I first heard this idea from Dr. R. Elisabeth Cornwell, an evolutionary psychologist. Dr. Cornwell has repeatedly offered this challenge in her classes. She first asks the men in the class to consider this hypothetical: leaving out women with whom they have some prior relationship or flirtation, could any one of them persuade a woman in the class to have sex with him prior to midnight that night? If successful, the man would get a million dollars, but if he failed, he would have to pay a million dollars. Of course, no force or coercion of any kind can be contemplated. The man cannot offer the woman a cut of the proceeds or even hint at any financial gain. This is all down to persuasion.

I've tried Dr. Cornwell's hypothetical in my talks around the country, and, when I pose the question, the males look about sheepishly, sometimes forlorn, but only rarely does a male raise his hand. Women tend to find this result most amusing, particularly when the same hypothetical is posed to them. Why? Well . . .

Knowing the predisposition of males toward sexual offers, women consistently raise their hands in far greater numbers than men. Women, and men, tend to get a good laugh at the expense of the hapless and predictable male of our species, while they both acknowledge a sociological truth. Women are less inclined to say "yes" when it comes to this subject and men are much less inclined to say "no." This reality is neither praised nor condemned. We simply recognize, with many exceptions, a general tendency. It is a marked gender difference. As Dr. Cornwell puts it, women tend far more than men to be the "gatekeepers" of sex. Women tend to think long term and, with exceptions of course, generally see long-term partnerships as a higher priority than a fling. It may be that, as sexism fades, there will be less stigma to women initiating sexual advances, but these are the results for now.

I'm a feminist not because women and men have no differences—we do. I'm a feminist because neither gender is superior or inferior to the other. I keep a poster of my hero Eleanor Roosevelt on my office wall because she was such a great human being. It was her actions, the choices that she made, and the policies she pursued that made her such a wonderful example to us all. Her gender and her sexuality were not the defining aspects of her greatness. And as the torture-endorsing Eva Peron and Margaret Thatcher demonstrate, no gender is perfect.

As a feminist myself, I'm confident most feminists don't agree with the extreme views expressed by Andrea Dworkin, who said, "Intercourse is the pure, sterile, formal expression of men's contempt for women." She also said, "I think that men will have to give up their precious erections and begin to make love as women do together." Sheesh. Talk about lack of inclusiveness.

So when do we get to the part where we all just lighten up about sex? The angry condemnations regarding sex, from the Right and the Left, are prissy, prudish, harsh, and humorless. And these condemnations, these sexual police brigades, are at the heart of fundamentalism and some forms of political correctness.

Better to accept the opposite sex as fellow human beings, wildly imperfect though we may be. Among any civilized people, regardless of one's predilections, no means no. Consequences, including, in many cases, prison, is the proper result for those who don't take no for an answer. Everyone must understand that, while flirtation is one of life's most enjoyable activities, no must be accepted with aplomb. But we still need to lighten up and let people—gay or straight, man or woman—be who they naturally are. We also need to understand that "who you are" can never include coerciveness, or expectations of privilege.

Passion with Good Humor, Candor without Sexism

Now, back to the early 1960s and Don Draper. The Don Draper character is tall, dark, and handsome, but he is often just plain dark. Even so, many women throughout America find something compelling—and alluring—about this character. The blogosphere brims with interest, expressed by women, regarding Don Draper. Why? Perhaps it's in part because Don Draper for all his blatant faults avoids the disingenuous and oily posing in which many men indulge ("Me? Think of sex? Oh, no. Not me!")

But there is something more that Draper displays: skill. We are, all of us—in a way that goes beyond the sexual—attracted to skill. *Mad Men* would simply be a soap opera were it not that the writers show us that Don Draper cares about his skill as an ad man and strives for high-quality work.

Think of Joan Baez, queen of folk. Her ability to attract men and women during the folk era was legendary. She had a magnetism that was Draper-like. (Although men go for the visual more, accomplishment matters to us as well.) And who did Joan Baez pick? For whom did she write the great torch song "Diamonds and Rust"? Dylan, of course—not exactly a man with matinee-idol good looks, but one of unique skill.

Draper and Dylan lead me to King and Kennedy—two other iconic males of the 1960s who, like Dylan, demonstrated remarkable skill. Songwriting and speechwriting are topics that have fascinated me since childhood. A well-crafted speech is like a beautiful pop song. Concise and punchy—with numerous "hooks" and artful phrasing that combine with a mood and feel that spark in the listener an increased and surging sense of passion. I collect speeches like other people collect coins or shot glasses and, for me, the summer of 1963 stands out. The summer of 1963 is to speechmaking what the summer of 1949 is to baseball.

In the summer of 1963 President Kennedy delivered his famed "Berlin Wall" speech, which called for freedom for all people, not merely freedom from Communism. That same summer, his speech on civil rights was correctly lauded by Dr. Martin Luther King as the first clear moral call from a president for racial justice. And Kennedy delivered his exceptional "We Are All Mortal" speech at American University, calling—successfully—for the first major step toward nuclear disarmament with the Nuclear Test Ban Treaty. Then, on August 28, 1963, Dr. King delivered his stunningly brilliant "I Have a Dream" speech. All of these speeches will stand for all time, in terms of writing, reasoning, and delivery.

Now to a little secret about these skillful men: you may have heard that Kennedy was rather friendly with a number of women, but you may—in fact—not have heard (perhaps because of political correctness) that Dr. King had similar friendships with women. Like Don Draper, these men shared an unapologetic frankness in approaching women and, truth be told, a number of sophisticated, educated women welcomed these advances. You can condemn these men—or condemn the women—but they were consenting adults, not children—and they did not partake in hypocritical lectures about sex.

Unlike Don Draper, Kennedy and King used their superlative skill to advance causes we as a people find deeply ennobling. Their skill was energizing, and, yes, attractive—in a very positive way.

It is the purview of women to decide what to do with their own response to whatever skills males display, and vice versa. Similarly, we must understand men and their behavior for what it more typically is—not what we might pretend that it should be. The same holds true for understanding women. Assent is never required, but understanding can't hurt. Let's not get so all-fired mad at people for being human. Gossips and name callers should be forcefully reminded by all to mind their own business.

Perhaps the greatest wisdom on this topic is to laugh together, men and women, about our human foibles and show affection for each other despite all our "naughty" predilections and to give sanctimonious condemnation a much-needed rest. Do women today long for the times of Don Draper and his early sixties sexism? Certainly not. Men shouldn't either. Yet there is a longing today for more candidness and less cornball political correctness—which can border on Victorian drivel. In our times, it may be possible to revive a refreshing candor while unequivocally rejecting outdated sexism and coerciveness. Can we dare to hope that Americans will finally lighten up and laugh a little more (or a lot more) about sex? If sexual choices between consenting adults are kept within the bounds of good will, let us not condemn our instinctual actions and reactions that long predate the gossips and grouches of all political stripes.

And I'm not just speaking about the Religious Right here. Many liberals today—in their rush to be politically correct—often seem most uncomfortable with acknowledging human beings for being human. Punishing people of either gender for sex, making people feel guilty for sex, is, as the blogger Greta Christina puts it, like "punishing you for getting hungry."

Notes Katie Roiphe in a July 2010 *New York Times* article, Don Draper exudes a skilled candor, a bold spontaneity, that, for all his evil ways, makes us in our present zeitgeist feel a twinge of discomfort. Draper wears crisp, well-tailored suits, but there's risk just under the surface. There's an old-school reserve, yet the real possibility that there will be a tumble into bed that wasn't calendared a week in advance. We twenty-first-century Americans live in times compartmentalized and tidy, calendared and subject to endless strategic planning meetings. Wild office parties? We're too busy looking at other people's lives on Facebook. Fun flirtation? That's for the Europeans. Drinking at the office party? We've got to get to the garden supply and buy mulch for our perfectly arranged yards, and choose the right shade of accent paint for our well-appointed den. Don Draper, with his many faults, seems to live energetically—in the present. That's magnetism.

Don Draper is different from us in all our hyperarranged "busyness." And, for more noble reasons, but with similar style, King and Kennedy are different from us today. They wore the suits, the conservative ties. They didn't share their feelings, yet they displayed their passions and they acted on those passions in every aspect of their lives. They fascinate and inspire us to this day.

Within American life in the twenty-first century—so tidy, so organic foods, so arranged, so scheduled, and so planned—there is this call in the heart for something impulsive, sexual, unplanned—something grabbed just for that moment of intensity, right away without hesitation. The passion to be skillful and the passion to be fully alive are closely intertwined.

Sex has become America's great sleight of hand. It is the bait and switch. The Meese Commission of the Ronald Reagan years lied about the connection between porn and violence, because those at the top really want us to focus on the easily understood trivia of Victorian sexual regulation rather than the complexities of the common good for an entire nation.

This prudish obsession with sex emanates from something inside that is twisted, dark, and vicious. Take a step back and survey the scene from Prop 8 in California or the attempts to gut Planned Parenthood in Washington, DC. Is there anyone more sex-crazed than a fundamentalist? We cannot allow the veneer of propriety to hide the truth: the old sexual attitudes really are poison. People get hurt by sexist laws and malicious Victorian gossip dressed as political correctness.

We must embrace the science of our sexual behavior, though being honest about our sexuality is not the same as being crass. Science cannot, and should not, justify male privilege nor adolescent ogling of women. Science can and should justify understanding and openness and acceptance and compassion, and maybe a little flirting every once in a while. What the hell.

Flirting is a joyous activity. Think about the last time you did it, and you may agree. It is an activity entirely consistent with moral values—and human nature. In those cases where it happens to lead to something more, well, we don't need pinch-lipped gossipy prudes regulating our bedrooms like referees with whistles at a football game.

The Morality of Conscience

For all their very human behavior, Kennedy and King—with refreshing vigor—understood real morality and spoke for morality at its most essential and its most vital. They exuded passion. We should thank them for that, not spend time nosing around in private places to which we were not invited. This repugnant obsession among those on the Right (and on the hyper–politically correct Left) with sexual trivia is deeply immoral because it distracts us from the real moral issues.

Lies about sex education and restrictions on women's health care are harmful to people and they are also bad public policy. The prude police are also very harmful to society as a whole because false religiously biased genital morality dominates American debate—and distracts the American people from the challenging and important moral issues of justice and compassion for our fellow citizens and for people throughout the world.

As a politician, I knew the guys who lobbied for companies that pollute, for tobacco companies that kill, for the alcohol companies that market to children. While it is socially acceptable, even brag worthy for some, to be a mouthpiece for a tobacco company, a polluter, a corporate exploiter of children, society can still make women and men uncomfortable with what the statistics say are normal and harmless sexual urges.

I remember in private practice being appointed by the court to represent a child rapist. I walked down the street about one block from the courhouse to the home of the victim. Entering the apartment where the little girl lived, I was struck with a sickly sweet smell of unclean neglect. The apartment was dirty, as was this little girl. The sheetrock in her apartment wall was broken open, cold air streamed in from a Maine winter. The neglect this child experienced in this home spoke of a harsh life that long predated her hideous rape. I then walked a few steps down the same street to the home of the young man who had raped her. My client's actions can never be excused, but his life can be examined realistically. He was a young man of about twenty with a mental disability. His parent's apartment had the same sickly sweet smell of dirty neglect. None of this excused his conduct, but the impact of seeing both these lives has never left me. There are larger issues that must be addressed, societal issues that require more effort, thought, and long-term thinking than one sanction for one crime can remedy. A greater moral vision is needed for the many children living in the most vulnerable of homes.

Moral is the right word. Morality should govern our actions. The morality of which I speak is the morality of conscience, not the morality of the mob nor the petty morality of the sexual gossip. The mob shouted out Bible passages to justify slavery. The mob thought we should burn alleged witches as friends of the devil. The mob thought innocent lives should be ruined to defend against godless Communism.

I was once scolded when speaking before a secular humanist group for using the word "morality," because, an audience member said, morality was a word for the fundamentalists. I disagree. I say the word morality has been stolen from us and we must take it back. When I served on the judiciary committee in Maine's legislature, we dealt with such issues as a woman's right to choose, discrimination based on sexual orientation, and child sex abuse and sex-crime law in general. Indeed, I chaired a sex-crime commission, and we successfully changed laws to better protect children who cannot consent.

In the midst of these efforts and successes, I'd inevitably have fundamentalist activists lobbying me with heavy use of the word "moral" as they wagged a finger at me. The implication was that I was immoral because I didn't think the sex lives of gay people was any of my business—nor the government's business—and because I didn't condemn women for their private sexual choices.

No matter what you might think about their own sense of morality, fundamentalists are very involved in the political process. They are passionate and vocal. Are you passionate about secular advocacy? Are you vocal?

Let's be passionate and vocal about allowing consenting adults to make their own decisions, and if they decide to indulge with gusto, so be it. If you lack moderation in eating, it will increase your risk of heart disease, diabetes, and cancer. But what is it exactly that happens when you enthusiastically enjoy protected sex? Your smile muscles are sore? Here's an idea: let's be more honest, and less Victorian, about our urges. And for gosh sakes, let's lighten up.

Let's celebrate sex, not because we are immoral but because we are moral.

And above all, let's work for a new sexual revolution—a revolution with no sexist overtones, a revolution filled with understanding, understanding between men and women, straight and gay, an understanding founded on our common humanity and an extra dose of good humor. When we reach that last day we will look back fondly on moments that were spontaneous, passionate, and full of laughter. To quote George Bernard Shaw, "I rejoice in life for its own sake. Life is no 'brief candle' for me. It is a sort of splendid torch which I have got hold of for the moment, and I want to make it burn as brightly as possible before handing it on to future generations."

Too many Americans have been hoodwinked into joining a huckster preacher in pointing an accusing finger at some alleged Hester Prynne in our midst. To make matters worse—it's a good bet the huckster's other hand is on their wallet.

5 Two American Traditions

Religious Hucksters and Secular Innovators

There are hundreds and hundreds of scientists, many of them holding Nobel Prizes, who believe in intelligent design.

—Michele Bachmann

There is nothing which can better deserve our patronage than the promotion of science and literature. Knowledge is in every country the surest basis of public happiness.

—George Washington

In 1966 the managers of radio station KLUE in Plainview, Texas, decided they didn't like it when John Lennon said, "Christianity will go. It will vanish and shrink." So the station owners of KLUE organized a huge bonfire, burning hundreds of Beatles records. The next day KLUE was taken out by a huge lightning bolt! I don't believe in divine intervention, but I do enjoy a little irony every once in a while.

John Lennon had numerous unpleasant qualities. Lennon admitted to domestic violence at one point. Lennon could be an angry drunk, sometimes drug addled to the point of delusion, and a dabbler in the political fringes. Lennon could be neglectful, ungrateful, and sometimes downright mean to people who were devoted to him (his first wife, his oldest son, Brian Epstein, George Martin, even Paul McCartney without whom the sometimes-ornery Lennon would never have risen to his unparalleled heights). Lennon's thoughts on cigarettes and I Ching and many other topics were downright wacky. His worldview was arguably flawed, particularly for believers in capitalism like me, but—all that said—John Lennon stands as one of a handful of twentieth-century figures who will be remembered—and justly revered—five hundred years from now. One of many reasons is his brilliantly simple song "Imagine." In that song Lennon looked into the future. Imperfect as Lennon was, his song's simply stated vision of a more humanitarian society, a vision already widely embraced around the world, will guide us for centuries. And, the music that Lennon created, especially when working with McCartney—marked by its unparalleled innovation and sheer joyfulness—will reverberate well into the future.

As we shall see, Steve Jobs connects the values of the Beatles to the spirit of innovation, which I'll get to later in this chapter, but first let's talk hucksterism, innovation's parasitic opposite. After all, innovators must by definition actually follow through on ideas. New ideas require creativity. Hucksters needn't be bothered with all that. I'll begin with an unexpectedly related question: which do you like better, having sex or attending religious services? Now I'm not judging which is better, mind you. To each her own, I always say. I do want to make sure however that we all at least know the difference between having sex and attending religious services, a distinction some hucksters apparently find challenging.

The Theocratic Hucksters

Recently retired U.S. congressman Chip Pickering seemed to have had a little difficulty making a distinction between sexual relations and religious services while in office. This seems especially odd because Congressman Pickering attended Pentecostal services—you know, the type where participants speak in tongues, venomous snakes are sometimes prominent guests, and premarital sex and adultery are mortal sins. You may remember Congressman Pickering from the movie *Borat* in which he participates in a Pentacostal event at which Darwin is jeered.

While a member of Congress, Pickering lived at "C Street," a rooming house in Washington, DC, affiliated with "The Family"—a seven-decade-old religious organization that is one of the most powerful and highly connected in the United States. C Street has been a home for many oh-so-impoverished "spiritual" members of Congress. Oh, wait, did I say rooming house? I meant to say church. You see, C Street receives tax deductions as a church that claims to hold "services" in Washington, DC.

Congressman Pickering was enjoying services alright. Congressman Pickering may well have shouted "Oh God" for all I know—but these are not the kind of services warranting a property-tax exemption.

But . . . sweet deal for The Family and Congressman Pickering! Congressman Pickering, partly because of C Street's religious-service tax exemption, paid about half what I pay for my DC-area apartment—and I live almost an hour from Capitol Hill, while C Street is prime Washington real estate. My place doesn't have partial maid service, effectively subsidized by Pickering's secretive elite religious sponsors. (I really should have talked to my landlord about the availability of a secretive elite religious power group. You can cut down on rent—and achieve eternal salvation.)

Congressman Pickering wasn't the only tenant who benefited from cheating the taxpayers. C Street, aka the Prayboy Mansion, also happened to be the home to such paragons of virtue as Governor Mark Sanford and Senator John Ensign. These three all managed to earn an "A" but, in their case, the letter had more to do with Nathaniel Hawthorne than Bible study achievement. Come to Jesus, baby! Austin Powers, while perhaps sartorially challenged, displays more honesty and heart than these oily characters.

The Family founded the National Day of Prayer. Its "theology" asserts that powerful people (I'm not making this up) are anointed by God and are subject to different rules than the rest of us. And The Family clearly practices the double-standard they preach. If you aren't powerful, you aren't anointed. Too bad for you.

Speaking of family, Congressman Pickering was a very vocal family-values politician. His "family values" included opposing a woman's right to choose, imposing a nationwide federal mandate to "protect" marriage from those nasty gay invaders, and, get this, voting to impeach Bill Clinton for his adultery. Since the religious "services" Congressman Pickering received at C Street were not from his wife, my generally libertarian sensibilities about sex are a tad offended here by the blatant hypocrisy. You didn't catch John F. Kennedy lecturing us about our sex lives.

What C Street was doing (claiming religious services when it operated primarily as subsidized housing for the privileged) wasn't strictly, uh, legal. Sanford, who benefited from C Street's subsidized housing while congressman, later sought counseling from his C Street pals, when, as South Carolina governor, his actions led to the colorful euphemism "hiking the Appalachian Trail"—now defined as canoodling with a woman in Brazil. There seems to be a pattern with these "family values" C Street residents. I could not give two hoots if people "get biological" or "jiggy" or both, but might it be possible to spare us the hypocrisy?

More scary than illegal activities by religious groups are some of the things that are entirely legal.

The Televangelist Hucksters

C Street may represent an unorthodox use of religious tax advantages (part of the rooming house's exemption was later revoked to reflect its residential use), but there are several unique tax loopholes in law that are clearly, if unethically, authorized by IRS code. For example, federal tax law permits churches and other religious organizations to give tax-free housing allowances to ministers, yet the ministers still get a deduction on their mortgage interest payment. It's a beautiful double dip.

Eight people, for example, secured the godly benefit of an income-tax-exempt housing allowance at Reverend Robert Schuller's Crystal Cathedral in Southern California. Three received housing allowances of more than $100,000. Three happened to be relatives of . . . Reverend Schuller.

For example, Carol Milner, Reverend Schuller's daughter, received a housing allowance. She bought a house later valued at $2.29 million. I don't know how many homes Carol Milner owns, but isn't it blessed that the taxpayers helped subsidize at least one of them. Keeping up with a mortgage is indeed a burden, and, of course, we taxpayers absolutely must pitch in and do our part to help godly people like Reverend Schuller and his daughter. This is one area where government has taken a very active role in protecting people in the housing crisis. What? You're not a megaminister? Or the family member of a preacher? Well, bad planning on your part.

The Prosperity Gospel is the "theology" that God provides material benefit to those he favors. Joyce Meyer has been a leading proponent of the Prosperity Gospel, and this "theology" has worked extremely well for her. You may have heard old-fashioned talk about living simply, but the Prosperity Gospel holds that God rewards those who pray—for houses or new cars or, one preacher actually said this, good seating at a restaurant.

Meyer, perhaps the top female evangelical preacher in America, brings in over $100 million annually to her ministry. When she talks the Prosperity Gospel, she lives it: "There's no need for us to apologize for being blessed." Referring to herself in the third person, Meyer says, "She has helped so many people!" She asks, "Is there no reward for anybody that's doin' what I'm doing?" Clearly we aren't worrying enough about whether Meyer is sufficiently rewarded. Luckily, God has provided some specific answers to Preacher Meyer's question. One answer is a multimillion-dollar private jet, because flying commercial is so, to quote Meyer, "uncomfortable" today.

Meyer prays that what people give to her ministry will—at some unspecified later date—"come back to them many times over." In other words, she takes their cash right now and assures the faithful that God will reimburse them at some unspecified future date. Poor Bernie Madoff is in jail. Had Madoff only mentioned that God would arrange his client's return on investment, he'd have his own TV show now.

Meyer's TV commercials invest millions to praise, well, Joyce Meyer for her ministry's foreign aid (and, of course, to ask for more money). In fact, only about $14 million of the $100 million it receives annually is reportedly spent on humanitarian aid (and some of that $14 million goes to proselytizing rather than to actual aid). Luckily we have her big money TV commercials to remind us of the holiness of Meyer's proselytizing "foreign aid." These ads (paid for with tax-deductible contributions of course) also conveniently remind us to give Joyce Meyer's ministry more money.

American taxpayers subsidize Joyce Meyer's jet, and her ministry in general, in the sense that contributions to her ministry are tax deductible—but Lord praise all of you—because you taxpayers really go the extra mile to subsidize houses for megaministers through the tax-free housing allowance. Like some of the wealthiest of the wealthy megaministers, Reverend Meyer may no longer even use the housing allowance because her ministry has already secured such vast wealth that the bad publicity may not be worth the exemption. (I'd need to see Joyce Meyer's tax return to know which deductions she actually takes.) That said, it's reassuring to know that our government makes these tax-free housing allowances available to all those ministers still struggling to become wealthier. There is no upper limit on the extravagance of a house eligible for this exemption.

Joyce Meyer has some spectacular competition when it comes to ministerial wealth. For example, Joel Osteen, pastor of Lakewood Church in Houston, possibly America's largest congregation, is famous for at least appearing to cry during his sermons. He has a lot to cry about. As Barbara Ehrenreich describes in her book *Bright-Sided*, Joel Osteen and his co-pastor wife Victoria Osteen have, like Joyce Meyer, suffered terribly at the hands of commercial airlines. The Osteens made the mistake of slumming without a private jet, actually being so humble—Christ-like, one might say—as to fly first class to Vail, Colorado, for a ski trip. (Now that's mixing with the rabble.)

Tragically, Victoria Osteen was aghast to find a stain, according to court records, about the size of a quarter, on her first-class seat's armrest. You can imagine how poor Victoria Osteen felt. To quote Lady Macbeth, "Out damn spot!" When the flight attendant did not respond immediately to Queen Victoria's complaint, Victoria did the only reasonable thing. She made her anger extremely clear to the flight attendant and then attempted to storm the cockpit demanding justice.

Who can blame Queen Victoria? She was flying first class after all. However, even first-class passengers must obey FAA regulations. Those ungrateful bureaucrats imposed a $3,000 fine on Victoria (something akin to a $20 fine for the average American). The flight attendant, perhaps smelling a little Prosperity Gospel herself, brought a suit against Victoria Osteen. Witnesses in the civil litigation described Victoria's behavior as that of a "combative diva." Still, the jury ruled in Victoria's favor. The FAA had already punished her cockpit tantrum, and Victoria had only yelled at the flight attendant. She hadn't, in fact, hit the flight attendant.

Naturally, the Osteens devoted their next sermon to their agonizing suffering at the hands of first-class flight attendants. Joel Osteen said, "It's not just a victory for us, it's a victory for God's kingdom." And "God is against those who are against us." Read those quotes again, just to let them sink in. "God is against those who are against us"—in a lawsuit about Victoria screaming at (but not hitting) a flight attendant? Then Victoria came on stage before the gathered throng at the church. Queen Victoria literally jumped up and down in a victory dance declaring, "I place a banner of victory over my head."

With such divine glory, you can understand why people voluntarily give millions to the Osteens. But if you despair at the thought of the poor elderly couples who give away their last dime to snake-oil salesmen, don't worry. Conveniently, politicians and the IRS have made sure that *all* us Americans do our part to help ministers get wealthy. We are so lucky. The IRS just hands our money to ministers without us needing to take all that time to write out a check. It makes it so convenient for us to do God's will.

You see, unlike your home, a preacher, no matter how wealthy, is eligible for the same huge tax-free housing allowance I've already described. The Osteens own a 5,000-square-foot home valued at over $1 million. Because of the vast wealth and fame that the Osteens have accumulated, they can now, ever-so-humbly, live off the fat of their products (which their fundamentalist-industrial complex so relentlessly promotes) and forgo the housing exemption. But what if this tax subsidy helped enrich their family in past years? Indeed, Osteen's father was a megaminister before him. Could we get our tax dollars back with interest? Using that old Prosperity Gospel, Victoria even convinced Joel to buy a more "elegant" house, because Victoria spoke words of "faith and victory" to Joel—about a bigger house. Joel says they would not have bought the bigger house had Victoria not talked him into "enlarging my vision." "God has so much more in store for you." Gandhi had nothing on these "divine" beings (particularly if you check out their MTV-worthy crib).

God has apparently made sure that the IRS views the megaministers as more equal than the rest of us in other ways too:

- Unlike nonprofits, churches don't have to file 990 forms (a basic financial disclosure). Thus, their finances are the most secretive of any so-called charitable organization. For-profit businesses, of course, must file detailed tax documents. So must 501(c)(3) non-profits. Because the finances of religious organizations are akin to the proverbial black box, it is difficult to even find out whether some-thing improper has occurred.

- Only a "high-level" IRS official can even authorize an audit of a religious organization. Meanwhile, the rest of us—whether individuals, for-profit businesses, or secular nonprofits—can be audited by any old IRS bureaucrat.

- Religious groups can legally give tax-free housing allowances to so-called clergy (some of whom just might be family), allowances that are not counted as income, exempting the housing from taxation.

Rick Warren, the multimillionaire megaminister (the one who believes that Jews will go to hell for not being Christian) managed to set up a sweet deal for himself. He got a tax-free housing allowance greater than the fair market value of his opulent home. And we're not talking about some shack. Back in 1994 his actual annual housing expenses were $76,309 (more than the cost of many homes, especially in 1994). But Rick Warren wanted even more, so the church paid him $86,175 as a so-called housing allowance—all of it tax free. The pesky IRS actually pointed to the law, and poor Rick Warren had to be satisfied with a fair market tax-free housing allowance, the mere $76,309. As law professor Erwin Chemerinsky wrote, "not only did [the Warrens] exempt hundreds of thousands of dollars in income from taxes in the first instance, but they were also able to deduct mortgage interest payments that they made with these tax-free dollars." Warren had done this for years.

Later, when Reverend Warren was more famous, he made quite the show of tithing from his income and forgoing church compensation. What Rick Warren conveniently fails to mention is the decades of wealth he accumulated in houses and property that he now already owns—thanks in large part to you the taxpayer. Only after that accumulation of wealth at taxpayer expense, and only after his religious enterprises have promoted his book sales to a fare-thee-well, did Warren do a (very successful) publicity splurge about not taking a salary and tithing. (Luckily, his church still acts like a marketing firm for his best sellers.) Ah, well, at least we know the nonreligious (and the Hindus, Buddhists, etc.) got the chance to subsidize Mr. Warren's rise to great wealth—before we all go to hell with the Jews.

In 1970 there were fewer than fifty so-called megachurches in the United States whose weekly attendance exceeded two thousand congregants. Often a megachurch boasts more than one minister eligible for a tax subsidy from your pocket. Today there are over two thousand such churches, with many churches boasting congregations many times larger than two thousand members.

There are certainly well-meaning clergy leaders out there, but word has indeed gotten around that a megaminister can pull in serious booty. In fact, a church with a mere 250 to 500 members might be worth a sweet crib or a Cadillac or two. Have you seen what the megaminister McMansions look like in your area? Have you asked to see their tax records? Remember there are often multiple parsonage homes per megachurch. And don't forget the homes of the leaders' children, siblings, and cousins who have been called to offer God's word and just happen to live in a tax-exempt residence. Most will not be as "prosperous" as the Osteens or Joyce Meyer, but thousands are now doing quite well thank you—with the help of your tax dollars.

The fact that Victoria Osteen behaved in a rude and self-aggrandizing manner and the fact that Joel Osteen is a tear-gushing smoothy are noteworthy facts because these characteristics are emblematic of the American huckster tradition gone wild. The "duke and dauphin," the con men who meet Huck and Jim on the Mississippi, would have been delighted had they been able to parlay their native huckster gifts into a government-sanctioned enterprise, subsidized by the IRS code, and offered the oily veneer of respectability.

The Prosperity Gospel clearly makes people like the Osteens and Joyce Meyer very prosperous indeed, but as Kevin Phillips, the fiscally conservative Republican author, writes, the Prosperity Gospel is having a *detrimental* effect on hundreds of thousands of average people who give to the likes of the Osteens. While the Osteens and their ilk rake it in preaching the Prosperity Gospel, countless Americans, believing in that gospel, assume mortgages they cannot afford and debts they simply can't pay back.

Kevin Phillips preaches something you don't hear much from Republicans anymore: actual fiscal conservatism. Giving money to the big ministers and praying for success with risky loans and faith in a Prosperity Gospel does not sit well with a true conservative. The Prosperity Gospel has been marketed professionally and has perhaps affected behavior on a scale like never before, but this insidious creed has deep roots.

Just as intelligent design is creationism by another name, the Prosperity Gospel is the modern descendant of not only traveling snake-oil salesmen but also Norman Vincent Peale's "power of positive thinking." A close friend of Richard Nixon and Billy Graham, Peale believed that, rather than working *with* your fellow human beings to solve problems, the average person needs to submissively change his or her attitude *about* problems and not actively focus on addressing the actual substance of the problems. You see, the average person should submissively change his or her attitude rather than be assertive or collaborative when facing the evidence of a problem. After all, the key—for the "little people" anyway—is to get rewarded after you are dead.

The Innovators

Now, for an entirely different attitude, consider the first person to win a Nobel Prize in two separate fields: Marie Curie. Madame Curie believed neither in a deity nor an afterlife. But Curie believed strongly that people "share a general responsibility for all humanity, our particular duty being to aid those to whom we think we can be most useful."

Einstein said that Marie Curie was someone who was never corrupted or seduced by the fame she earned for her groundbreaking research in chemistry and physics—research that later saved lives through its use in cancer treatment. Marie Curie never became as full of herself, never felt as worthy of queenly attention as, for example, a Victoria Osteen.

Madame Curie said, "I was taught that the way of progress is neither swift nor easy." Praying for prosperity? Not enough. Relying on a preacher to pray for your success? That was not the Curie approach.

Marie Curie, the first woman ever awarded a PhD in all of Europe, said, "I never see what has been done; I only see what remains to be done."

Curie also said, "Scientific work . . . must be done for itself, for the beauty of science. . . . then there is always the chance that a scientific discovery may become, like radium, a benefit for humanity."

This nonbeliever was a great believer in human collaboration and in science for the sake of science: "science has great beauty. A scientist in the laboratory is not only a technician [but] a child placed before natural phenomena which impress . . . like a fairy tale." But this "fairy tale" does not reject inquiry. This great beauty encourages inquiry. Science welcomes skepticism—not gullibility.

Marie Curie had a different philosophy than the "power of positive thinking" and its vapid intellectual descendant, the Prosperity Gospel. Curie sought to improve our shared world, not pretend the world is different from what evidence tells us it is. Curie said, "Life is not easy for any of us. . . . We must have perseverance. . . . We must believe that we are gifted for something and that this thing must be attained." Curie's focus was not on the temporary prosperity of acquiring things for herself—but on the greater goal of achieving progress for all.

Now consider the second and only other person to have been awarded a Nobel Prize in two different fields: Linus Pauling. Aside from their two Nobel Prizes, Curie and Pauling shared something else in common: both rejected supernatural beliefs. This may seem like a coincidence, but in fact it's typical among scientists. A recent survey by the National Academy of Sciences found that 79.0 percent of physical scientists identify themselves as atheist, and 76.3 percent do not believe in an afterlife. Like Curie, Pauling's lack of religion seems to have enhanced his highly moral world-view. Linus Pauling thought the Golden Rule needed editing: "Do unto others 20 percent better than you would expect them to do unto you, to correct for subjective error."

Pauling's first Nobel Prize was for his scientific research. Francis Crick called Pauling the "father of molecular biology," stating that his work would "save lives for generations to come." Pauling's second Nobel Prize was for his efforts to promote peace through the banning of nuclear tests. By contrast President George W. Bush famously pointed to the Book of Revelations regarding his decision to invade Iraq. This biblically inspired war-mongering approach to conflict, seen frequently in modern fundamentalism, is by definition not one you will find among secularists, especially not among those who've won two Nobel Prizes.

Linus Pauling earned a reputation for blunt straight talk. This noble American characteristic was shared by his more famous scientific colleague Thomas Edison—he of the phonograph, the light bulb, the motion picture camera, and the electric power plant—who said, "I never did a day's work in my whole life. It was all fun." Edison also said, "I cannot believe in the immortality of the soul. . . . No, all this talk of an existence for us, as individuals, beyond the grave is wrong."

With his direct, plain-spoken pragmatism, Edison is a quintessentially American genius who transformed the uses of electricity. Edison is an intellectual descendent of that other American genius scientific tinkerer, Ben Franklin. Franklin is responsible for many of the basic discoveries and even terms that we still use today in discussing electricity, such as "positive" and "negative" and "electric motor." Franklin said, "I have found Christian dogma unintelligible. Early in life, I absented myself from Christian assemblies."

Franklin, Edison, and Pauling all spoke for a deep current in American thought that takes great joy in learning about our world as it is and working with others to improve it.

Franklin was also deeply involved in politics. His religious skepticism was almost as strong as that of Jefferson. The Founders, while specifically prohibiting a religious test for office and specifically prohibiting establishment of religion, specifically encouraged scientific and artistic progress and patent innovation in the Constitution's Article I, Section 8: "The Congress shall have Power . . . To promote the Progress of Science and useful Arts."

Apple Computers and Apple Records vs. the Shiny Shyster Charlatans

When faced with a challenging reality, it is not sufficient to merely emphasize changing your attitude so as to passively accept the reality, nor is it enough to pray. When faced with a challenging reality, we must actually do things to improve our world.

Steve Jobs once said, "Remembering that I'll be dead soon is the most important thing I've ever encountered to help me make the big choices in life, because almost everything—all external expectations, all pride, all fear of embarrassment or failure—these things just fall away in the face of death, leaving only what is truly important. Remembering that you are going to die is the best way I know to avoid the trap of thinking you have something to lose. You are already naked. There is no reason not to follow your heart."

When it comes to innovation, developing those tools and gadgets we all love to use, Jobs chooses to emulate none other than the Fab Four: "My model for business is the Beatles. They were four guys who kept each other's negative tendencies in check. They balanced each other and the total was greater than the parts. And that's how I see business. Great things in business are never done by one person, they are done by a team of people." Thus, Mr. Jobs eloquently summarizes an essential aspect of the humanist ideal.

The viewpoint that we work with our fellow human beings, and not in subservience to the supernatural, guides innovators like George Soros, Warren Buffett, Bill Gates, and Mark Zuckerberg. Unfortunately, America's political life is no longer dominated by the likes of Franklin, Jefferson, Madison, and Kennedy.

While demographics give me optimism that the Zuckerberg generation may lead us to a better future, there is an ominous disparity between the rationalism on the rise in our youth and the theocracy on the rise in our politics.

As discussed, extreme fundamentalist sexual dogma is imposed in American law in ways that lead to the discrimination of sexual minorities, the treatment of women as second-class citizens, and the promotion of unscientific sexual propaganda that hurts public health and increases unplanned pregnancy. Meanwhile, many of the ministers who preach that very dogma live luxuriously—subsidized by our tax money with special tax exemptions offered to no one else and required nowhere in the Constitution.

A for-profit business that actually creates something useful? No tax exemption for the housing expenses of its CEO—nor for any of his or her employees.

A secular nonprofit that focuses not on proselytizing but on, say, helping poor children? No tax exemption for the housing expenses of its executive director, nor for any staff.

A secular nonprofit that lobbies for the policy values of Secular Americans? Alas, no tax exemption for its executive director's home either. And, in seriousness, there shouldn't be such an exemption for anyone.

We do not sufficiently reward or value innovation in America today. Instead, we reward the shiny shyster charlatan. America's exceptional heritage is embodied by Franklin's boundless curiosity, Edison's endless tinkering, and Pauling's meticulous analysis. Our government and our culture today devalue these great American virtues.

In today's American culture, people often ask, what would Jesus do? But let's consider what Joel Osteen and his ilk actually do in the name of Jesus. Osteen asks for more money—right now—from parishioners with promises of wealth later in this life and salvation in the next. But the cash here and now helps promote products that benefit the wallet of . . . Joel Osteen. That's what Osteen and his antecedents have always done. Now they play the game with a multimedia sound stage, a topnotch Web site, heavy book promotion, and glossy brochures, but snake oil is snake oil no matter how pretty the bottle.

If innovation is the test, if facing difficult realities and making positive change is the test, we must remember that, all his marketing aside, Osteen's level of productivity remains nil, zip. What new product has Osteen created? What scientific breakthrough has Osteen achieved? Joel Osteen talks of miracles—but what new medical miracle has he produced?

Madame Curie? Ben Franklin? Thomas Edison? Linus Pauling? They faced the world as it is and used innovation and initiative to learn, to aspire, to collaborate, and to improve our shared human condition. The Osteens produce nothing.

"Carryin' Pictures of Chairman Mao"
In 1994 we witnessed Newt Gingrich's Contract with America. In 1995 Gingrich imposed the little-noticed—but watershed—death of the Office of Technology Assessment (OTA). The OTA was strictly nonpartisan and issued accurate and technical reports on science and technology on which elected officials and the public could rely for objective analysis. This office had successfully saved taxpayers money through suggesting greater efficiency, including early use of electronic tax filing.

The death of the OTA symbolizes the loss of scientific reasoning in American policy generally. We are no longer the America that challenges itself to go to the moon. We have not been inspired by great leaders who call us to sacrifice—and innovate—for the greater good.

I kidded earlier about the C Street group and its tax-subsidized housing and sexual shenanigans, but the history of The Family runs deep and dark. The Family's secretive leader, Doug Coe, positively compared Jesus's teachings to the Red Guard during the Chinese Cultural Revolution: "I've seen pictures of young men in the Red Guard of China. . . . they would bring in this young man's mother and father, lay her on the table with a basket on the end. . . . He would take an axe and cut her head off. . . . They have to put the purposes of the Red Guard ahead of the mother-father-brother-sister—their own life! That was a covenant. A pledge. That was what Jesus said."

Jeff Sharlet, author of *The Family*, documents Coe's positive comparison of the special privilege of The Family with the powers of Joseph Stalin and Adolf Hitler. The powerful inner circle of The Family, it seems, is anointed by God to do far more than merely commit adultery; according to the ministry's very theology, its elite has god-given license to do what would be immoral for others.

America can clog its intellectual arteries with the greasy words of religious hucksters out to pick vulnerable pockets, so as to enrich their privileged, tax-subsidized lives—or it can inspire people to work together in the best interests of our country and fellow citizens. We may have reason, science, and youth on our side, but people of a secular bent make a mistake in underestimating the theocrats and hucksters. Religious extremists are diligent and, as we shall see in the next chapter, after many years of hard work, their ranks in the highest corridors of power are greater than at any time in U.S. history. Yet we still have the power to "imagine" a better world, then work for it.

6 The Theocrats (aka the Fundamentalist Fifty)

The first job we have as Americans is to reach out to everybody in the country who is not yet saved, and to help them understand the spiritual basis of a creator-endowed society.
—Newt Gingrich

I don't have any respect for the Religious Right.
—Barry Goldwater

Do we have a theocracy in America? Not yet. But at no other time in American history have we had such a high percentage of theocratic members of Congress—people who expressly endorse religious bias in American law. Just as ominously, at no other time have religious fundamentalists effectively had veto power over one of the country's two major political parties. The religious bias in numerous laws described in this book is not the result of a constitutional requirement. Far from it. These biased laws have been enacted *despite* our Constitution.

There are only 535 members of Congress, and they make laws for the other 300 million of us. By definition, then, any single member of Congress holds huge power. To understand the scope of the overall threat posed by modern theocrats to the values of our Founders and our Constitution, let us look at the record and statements of the theocrats themselves.

Many—indeed, most—of the 535 sitting members of Congress who vote consistently for theocratic policies will not be discussed in the pages that follow. Doing so would take a whole book in itself. Rather, the fifty members of Congress listed in this chapter are merely a representative sampling of those politicians who wear their theocratic bias on their sleeve—ones worthy of an award for their commitment to theocratic values.

The separation of church and state is an issue that should transcend party—and it did in the past. Today we rarely find elected Republicans—politicians—who unequivocally support the separation of church and state. This was not the case forty years ago. The reality has changed. Most elected Republicans today would categorically reject the pungently stated sentiments of Barry Goldwater that introduce this chapter. For decades, Mr. Conservative embodied not merely Republican values but right-wing Republican values. The fact that Goldwater's views would make him persona non grata in the Republican Party today can be interpreted in only one way: it marks a seismic shift toward theocracy within the Republican Party.

Don't believe me? Enjoy sampling these heroes of twenty-first-century American theocracy. We must make our fellow citizens aware of the extremism of these high-ranking elected officials. Some statements quoted here (if they weren't coming from members of Congress) would be humorously loony. I think the Tinfoil Hat Award should go to Congressman Steve Pearce. But you may disagree. The competition is fierce, as you shall see. Many of the comments below relate to gay people, but this is because the issue of gay rights has gotten so much media attention that politicians are forced to reveal their attitudes toward the gay community—but their theocratic voting record extends far beyond any one issue.

The theocratic award winners listed here are listed alphabetically. Enjoy dipping your toe in the pool of theocracy, the water's warm, what with all the fire and brimstone underneath. Without further ado, I present the Fundamentalist Fifty Awards.

Winner: The Michigan-Is-Very-Scary Award
Congresswoman Sandy Adams (R-FL): Congresswoman Adams voted to enact burdensome waiting periods and tough parental notice laws for young women seeking abortions and voted to force women to have ultrasound tests before terminating a pregnancy. Congresswoman Adams opposes stem cell research and is proud that she "fought against this type of research funding in the Florida House of Representatives." She opposes teaching evolution and has voted for teachers to "teach theories that contradict the theory of evolution." She says that Christians should reject evolution in favor of "the biblical terms of how we came about." When asked whether she believed in evolution, Adams replied, "I'm Christian. What else do you want to know?" Adams supports Florida's unsuccessful private school vouchers program, including for religious schools, and wants to display the Ten Commandments in public schools. Congresswoman Adams claims, with no basis, that Islamic law (sharia) thrives in some towns in

Michigan and may spread: "The Muslim extremist project is to create pockets and to grow their Muslim extreme philosophies, and if you look at some of our towns within our own borders, like Michigan, Michigan has cities that have a lot of Muslim influence and even so much as I would say some extremist Muslim influence because they are trying to operate under sharia law, not American law."

Winner: The Mamma-Grizzly Award
Senator Kelly Ayotte (R-NH): Sarah Palin endorsed Ayotte, who agrees with Palin on women's rights and gay rights. Senator Ayotte says same-sex couples shouldn't be able to adopt.

Winner: The Protect-Us-from-the-Evolutionist-Cult Award
Congresswoman Michele Bachmann (R-MN), Constitutional Conservative Caucus and Tea Party Caucus Chair: Congresswoman Bachmann says believers in evolution represent a "cult following." In the Minnesota Senate, Bachmann supported teaching creationism in public schools. Bachmann states her work to block LGBT rights "is a very serious matter, because it's our children who are the prize for this community, they [gay people] are specifically targeting our children." She spearheaded a state constitutional amendment banning same-sex marriage. She referred to homosexuality as "personal enslavement." In Washington, Bachmann cosponsored a bill to give "14th Amendment protections to an embryo or fetus." Speaking to a fundamentalist group, she prayed God would "expand this ministry beyond anything that the originators of this ministry could begin to think or imagine." This fundamentalist group's leader described the execution of gays as a "moral" act since "homosexuality is an abomination," and later suggested that Muslim Americans and Minnesota congressman Keith Ellison, a Muslim, are planning on "overthrowing the United States Constitution" by "bring[ing] in Sharee [sic] law through the homosexual agenda." Huh?

Winner: The Caped-Crusader Award
Congressman Roscoe Bartlett (R-MD): Congressman Bartlett carried Rev. Sung Myung Moon's purple cape as Moon was literally crowned—yep, a religious leader crowned!—in a congressional building.

Winner: The War-on-Christmas-Concocted-Issue Award
Senator Roy Blunt (R-MO): Senator Blunt claimed, falsely, that the Employee Non-Discrimination Act (ENDA) would put people at legal risk

if they have a Bible in their work cubicle. He has also voted for government-imposed school prayer.

Winner: The William-Jennings-Bryan-Creationism-in-School Award
Congressman John Boehner (R-OH), Speaker: In 2002, Congressman Boehner wrote the Ohio Board of Education urging the teaching of creationism in public schools. Boehner has voted to ban same-sex couples from adopting and to repeal domestic partnership laws, and supports a constitutional amendment to ban same-sex marriage. Boehner has also voted against protecting reproductive health clinics and has backed laws compelling women and girls to go through biased "counseling" before terminating a pregnancy.

Winner: The 2012-Must-Be-the-Year-of-the-Koran Award
Congressman Paul Broun (R-GA): Congressman Broun took time to draft legislation calling for 2010 to be the year of the Bible. Broun "sponsored legislation to give human fertilized eggs the full legal protection afforded a person from the moment that a sperm penetrates the membrane of the egg cell."

Winner: The Demonic-Homosexual-Sodomites Award
Congresswoman Ann Marie Buerkle (R-NY): Congresswoman Buerkle denounced "demonic homosexual sodomites." A group she led has blocked access to a gynecologist's office, because some women dared to have abortions there. Congresswoman Buerkle once joined in an antichoice parade in which someone carried a dead fetus.

Winner: The The-First-Amendment-Isn't-for-You-People Award
Congressman Eric Cantor (R-VA), Majority Leader: Congressman Cantor opposed the proposed Islamic community center near Ground Zero: "Everybody knows America's built on the rights of free expression, the rights to practice your faith, but come on." Theocrats, it seems, have a selective view of religious freedom. While in office, Congressman Cantor has voted against every bill to fund stem cell research, calling this research a "distraction" that would lead to "embryo harvesting, perhaps even human cloning." With a 0.00 (zero) percent lifetime rating from NARAL Pro-Choice America and the Human Rights Campaign, Cantor supported the anti–abortion rights Stupak-Pitts Amendment in the 2010 health-care debate. Cantor voted against the Employment Non-Discrimination Act and supports a constitutional amendment to ban same-sex marriage.

Winner: The "Right"-to-Neglect-Children Award
Senator Dan Coats (R-IN): Senator Coats succeeded in allowing so-called faith healers to have greater leeway to medically neglect their children. Coats argued that child neglect of this type is a constitutional right. (Pssst, it's not.) Senator Coats is an adherent of the C Street–based Fellowship Foundation's extreme theology of power, the group exposed in Jeff Sharlet's book *The Family*. Coats has labeled Sharlet an enemy of Jesus.

Winner: The Crazed-Lesbians-on-the-Loose Award
Senator Tom Coburn (R-OK): Senator Coburn said a campaign worker told him "lesbianism is so rampant in some of the schools in southeast Oklahoma that they'll only let one girl go to the bathroom [at a time]." (Hearing this newsflash, teenage boys in southwest Oklahoma are driving east at top speed.) During the health-care debate, Coburn expressed his hope that a Democratic senator of the majority caucus would not be able to make the vote: "What the American people ought to pray is that somebody can't make the vote tonight. That's what they ought to pray."

Winner: The Box-Turtles-Are-Sexy-Too Award
Senator John Cornyn (R-TX): Consider this excerpt from an advance copy of a speech that Senator Cornyn was to give at the Heritage Foundation: "It does not affect your daily life very much if your neighbor marries a box turtle. But that does not mean it is right. . . . Now you must raise your children up in a world where that union of man and box turtle is on the same legal footing as man and wife." The best I can say here is that Senator Cornyn removed the reference to the box turtle in the actual speech, but it did earn him a *Daily Show* mention.

Winner: The No-Hussy-Teachers Award
Senator Jim DeMint (R-SC): Senator DeMint said single mothers who live with men should be barred from teaching. He later apologized, saying his remarks were "distracting from the main issues." DeMint has also said openly gay people shouldn't be allowed to teach in public schools. Although he has noted that this opinion reflects his personal values, and is not necessarily the basis for legislation, he opposes gay marriage because of the "costly secondary consequences" to society from the prevalence of certain diseases among homosexuals.

Winner: The Vote-against-Gay-People-Unless-They-Happen-to-Be-My, ahem, Chief-of-Staff Award

Congressman David Dreier (R-CA), Rules Committee Chair: Congressman Dreier voted against Housing Opportunities for Persons with AIDS, a program offering shelter for the impoverished sick. He voted against funding for a federal program that furnishes the poor with the AIDS medications they need to live. Dreier doesn't worry about health care for his male partner, the highest paid staffer on Capitol Hill at one point. Sweet Jesus! God apparently cares for gay people (who are well connected). Dreier voted to ban same-sex couples from adopting children and against reproductive choice.

Winner: The Anti-Anti-Christian Award

Congresswoman Renee Ellmers (R-NC): Reporter Anderson Cooper asked then-candidate Ellmers about her ad in which she condemned the construction of "victory mosques" in lands conquered by Muslims centuries ago and made an analogy between those mosques and the so-called Ground Zero Mosque. Cooper noted that Christians built churches in places they conquered, including Rome. Her reply? "I guess what I could ask you is, are you antireligion, are you anti-Christian in your thinking?"

Winner: The No-Buddha-Doorstop Award

Senator Mike Enzi (R-WY): With Senators DeMint and Vitter, Senator Enzi authored a bill to mandate that the U.S. Capitol Visitor Center always prominently display the words "Under God" and "In God We Trust," and that Capitol staff must allow and leave on display any other "Judeo-Christian" symbols prepared or produced for the visitor center. So, crosses and Torahs would be welcome, but Buddha doorstops? A no go. Senator Enzi also participates in The Family, the group whose prime organizer in Uganda was the politician who proposed legislation calling for the death penalty for homosexual conduct.

Winner: The Voice-of-God Award

Congressman Phil Gingry (R-GA): Congressman Gingry said in support of a federal constitutional ban on gay marriage: "I think God has spoken very clearly on this issue." It's so convenient when you hear directly from the boss.

Winner: The Congressman-Pearce-Wacky-Reasoning Award

Congressman Louis Gohmert (R-TX), Crime, Terrorism and Homeland Security Committee Chair: Congressman Gohmert has likened homosexuality to bestiality, pedophilia, and necrophilia. He opposes gay people serving openly in the military because gays "cannot control their hormones to the point that they are a distraction to the good order and discipline of the military." Speaking against hate-crime legislation, Gohmert asked, "You think a pregnant mother does not deserve the protection of a homosexual? You think a military member doesn't deserve the protection of a transvestite?" Huh? But "huh" can often come to mind with Congressman Gohmert. Consider this reasoning (I'll get back to religion, I promise, but indulge me because this one's so bizarre): Congressman Gohmert actually claimed that "terrorist cells overseas" were planning to bring pregnant women "into the United States to have a baby" so the babies could become citizens. "And then they would turn back where they could be raised and coddled as future terrorists," Gohmert explained, "and then one day, twenty, thirty years down the road, they can be sent in to help destroy our way of life." What a great movie pitch! The Manchurian fetus.

Winner: The Antiscience Award
Congressman Ralph Hall (R-TX), Science and Technology Committee Chair: Using deceptive procedural tactics, Congressman Hall sabotaged a bill intended to boost science jobs and education by attaching an irrelevant amendment about pornography. Astronomer and writer Phil Plait called Hall's move a "deplorable stunt" and "blatant partisan ploy." Hall has a top rating with Christian fundamentalists.

Winner: The Michele-Bachmann-Is-Moderate Award
Congresswoman Vicky Hartzler (R-MO): Congresswoman Hartzler supported legislation that "would have allowed for prosecutors to charge women who obtained late-term abortions with murder" and permit "second-degree murder charges to be filed against doctors who performed such procedures." Women who have late-term abortions usually do so because of a very serious health issue. She wrote a book for fundamentalist activists called *Running God's Way*. It discusses "Christian" ways to run for office and how to run a campaign "using events and stories in the Bible as a guide." Hartzler said her book provides candidates with "the tools and inspiration they need to bring God's light in a darkening world." She led the fight to stop Missouri from ratifying the Equal Rights Amendment for women.

Winner: The God-Bless-You Award
Congressman Wally Herger (R-CA): In 2009 Congressman Herger, a powerful ways and means committee member, attended a town hall meeting

where an audience member referred to himself as a "proud right-wing terrorist." Herger responded with, "Amen. God bless you. There goes a great American." Huh?

Winner: The Spreading-the-"Political-Philosophy-of-Jesus" Award
Senator Jim Inhofe (R-OK): Senator Inhofe first campaigned for his seat touting the slogan "God, Guns, and Gays." As Jeff Sharlet reported, Inhofe spent at least $187,000 of taxpayer money—not counting his military transportation cost—to meet with foreign leaders on behalf of The Family, the organization behind C Street. Inhofe's mission, he declared, was to use his status as a U.S. senator—and a Family brother—to spread the "political philosophy of Jesus, something put together by Doug." "Doug" is Doug Coe, long-time leader of The Family, who, according to Sharlet, has praised the leadership skills of Hitler. Inhofe claimed that, because the Bible says God gave the West Bank to Abraham, America is violating God's law with any policy other than one directed at eliminating Palestinians from all territory Abraham could have seen from Hebron 4,000 years ago.

Winner: The Being-"Profamily"-Means-Stealing-Cars-and-Lying-about-Your-Military-Record-Are-OK-so-Long-as-You-Are-Antichoice-and-Antigay Award
Congressman Darrell Issa (R-CA), Committee on Oversight and Government Reform Chair: Congressman Issa received a 100 percent "profamily" rating from Phyllis Schlafly's Eagle Forum. And why not? Haven't people in your family been brought up on gun charges (more than once)? And car theft charges (more than once)? Surely the fact that charges were brought more than once is simply evidence of a conspiracy born of antifamily nonbelievers. What of the allegations that Issa exaggerated his military record and falsely claimed service on presidential protection duty? Surely, lies from Wiccans and Satanists. After all, when someone has the Eagle Forum endorsement, one knows that one's "family values" remain absolute and one has the moral authority to lecture others.

Winner: The Way-Scarier-than-Stephen-King Award
Congressman Steve King (R-IA), Immigration Committee Chair: Congressman King has called Joe McCarthy "a hero for America." When asked at a rally in support of Arizona's immigration law if Obama was bringing "small quantities of Muslims into this country," King said he "wouldn't be surprised that that is the real factual basis." King said Democrats were like Pontius Pilate and would have supported the

pharaohs over Israelite slaves. On Glenn Beck's show, King said Democrats were trying to "take away the liberty that we have right from God" because Congress was voting on the health-care reform bill on a Sunday. King voted against allowing U.S. citizens and legal residents to petition for their permanent partners (including same-sex partners) to obtain U.S. residency or citizenship. King told the Family Research Council that gay Americans should stay in the closet if they wanted to avoid discrimination and equated gay rights with the rights of "unicorns and leprechauns." King has analogized homosexuality with incest and labeled marriage equality as "a purely socialist concept." King voted against a plaque commemorating slaves who helped build our nation's Capitol, labeling it part of a plot "by liberals in Congress to scrub references to America's Christian heritage from our nation's Capitol."

Winner: The Theocrat's Pharmacist Award
Congressman Raul Labrador (R-ID): Congressman Labrador has voted to legally authorize medical professionals to shirk their professional duties and refuse to fill valid prescriptions for contraceptives. He opposes abortion in all cases including rape and incest. Labrador voted to make the federal government "provide for the presence of God in the public domain." He wants to ban openly gay and lesbian soldiers from the military and opposes same-sex marriage.

Winner: The Other-51-Weeks-Must-Be-Muslim-Heritage-Weeks Award
Senator Joe Manchin (D-WV): Thanksgiving Week was proclaimed Christian Heritage Week in West Virginia by Manchin when he was governor.

Winner: The Domestic-Violence-Sensitivity Award
Congressman Alan Nunnelee (R-MS): Congressman Nunnelee voted to allow for fundamentalist-advocated covenant marriage, a marriage agreement that makes divorce very difficult (a brilliant idea in domestic violence situations). Nunnelee led a successful push making the DMV print "Choose Life" license plates, with the money going to antichoice groups. (I'm sure he'd be fine with a flying spaghetti monster license plate with proceeds going to a secular group. I'm serious, Mississippi friends. Ooh, or maybe a Wiccan license plate! If government says yes to one religious symbol, it must say yes to another.) Nunnelee "led the efforts to place our national motto, In God We Trust, on the wall of every school classroom in the state." He also is "proud to have pushed the statutory

language prohibiting same sex couples from adopting as well as the Constitutional Amendment prohibiting same sex marriage in [the Mississippi legislature]."

Winner: The Jim-DeMint-Isn't-Theocratic-Enough Award
Senator Rand Paul (R-KY): Senator Paul keynoted a Minnesota Constitution Party event. The Constitution Party's Web site proclaimed, "The goal of the Constitution Party is to restore American jurisprudence to its Biblical foundations. . . . The U.S. Constitution established a Republic rooted in Biblical law." Paul says he would "strongly support" court-stripping legislation "restricting federal courts from hearing cases like *Roe v. Wade*" and would back a "Sanctity of Life Amendment" that would define in law that life begins at conception. Paul thinks politicians should decide minority rights instead of the Constitution and says "you could have prayer in public schools." Paul declined to answer a question about the age of the earth. Rand Paul has said, "My goal is to make DeMint look like a moderate."

Winner: The Great "Libertarian" Award
Congressman Ron Paul (R-TX): Congressman Paul said, "The notion of a rigid separation between church and state has no basis in either the text of the Constitution or the writings of our Founding Fathers." He said our Founders envisioned an America with "churches serving as vital institutions that would eclipse the state in importance." Many young people are attracted to the libertarian veneer of Ron Paul's presidential campaigns. Let's examine his record: Paul introduced the Sanctity of Life Act, which would define human life as beginning at conception and remove challenges to prohibitions on abortion from federal court jurisdiction. In 2005 Paul introduced the We the People Act to disallow any claim based upon the right of privacy, including "any such claim related to any issue of . . . reproduction." Such a law would allow states to outlaw contraception. Talk about big government.

The perennial presidential candidate now says he was unaware of the bigoted rhetoric about African-Americans and gays appearing in his newsletters from the 1970s through the 1990s, though he claimed authorship at the time. One newsletter comment related to the Los Angeles riots: "Order was only restored in L.A. when it came time for the blacks to pick up their welfare checks"—a statement he now repudiates. Paul's newsletter opposed the Martin Luther King federal holiday. ("What an infamy Ronald Reagan approved it!" one newsletter complained. "We can thank him for our annual Hate Whitey Day.") A 1990s newsletter attacked the "X-Rated Martin Luther King" as a "world-class philanderer who beat up his paramours," "seduced underage girls and boys," and "made a pass at" fellow civil-rights leader Ralph Abernathy. (Martin Luther King slept with various adult women, but all the other allegations are vicious lies against one of our greatest Americans.) One Ron Paul newsletter stated that "opinion polls consistently show only about 5% of blacks have sensible political opinions" and that "if you have ever been robbed by a black teen-aged male, you know how unbelievably fleet-footed they can be." Many perceive Ron Paul as a great libertarian. Maybe God told him racism and theocracy are libertarian values.

Winner: The Tinfoil-Hat-Award
Congressman Steve Pearce (R-NM): Congressman Pearce says there are "serious downstream effects" to gay marriage: "They might think to themselves, 'I'm going to marry everyone in California with AIDS, then suddenly they've got access to maybe the benefit program, the health insurance." Yeah, he says that, um, stay with him here, gay marriage would lead to . . . polygamy . . . then, once there's polygamy, see, then some heathen would marry everybody in California with AIDS . . . and then—hold the phone!—then the unthinkable might result, people might actually have health-care benefits! OH, THE HUMANITY!! It's simple math: lickety-split you've got yer gay marriage then you've got yer polygamy then yer health coverage for people with AIDS. Luckily, the good congressman supports a constitutional amendment to ban gay marriage. Phew! Disaster averted. JE-sus! That was close.

Winner: The Let's-Not-Protect-against-HIV/AIDS-in-Africa Award
Congressman Joe Pitts (R-PA), Health Subcommittee Chair: Congressman Pitts, a leader of The Family of C Street fame, crafted a 2003 amendment to an HIV/AIDS funding bill, mostly directed toward Africa, that required 33 percent of the funding be used only for abstinence-until-marriage programming. Pitts also worked against condom distribution in Uganda. Jeff Sharlet, in his book, *The Family*, states that Congressman Pitts has contributed more to the increasing AIDS rate in Uganda than any other single person, reversing what had been a real success story in fighting HIV in the 1990s.

Winner: The Christocrat Award
Senator Ron Portman (R-OH): In 2005 Senator Portman sat at the head table at an organizing meeting for Rev. Rod Parsley's Patriot Pastors and

its effort to register 400,000 "values voters." (Even John McCain disavowed Parsley's endorsement.) At the event sponsored by Parsley's Center for Moral Clarity, Parsley declared himself a "Christocrat." Portman naturally said, "We are in the right place doing the right thing." He has a 100 percent antichoice record on abortion and a history of backing government-run school prayer, and he has voted to ban gay people in DC from adopting.

Winner: The Local-Control Award
Congressman Tom Price (R-GA): Price says, "Nothing can be more important than the sanctity of our families." How does Price plan to ensure this "sanctity"? Among other things, he wants the U.S. government to block the local government in Washington, DC, from allowing gay marriage.

Winner: The Senator-Who-Says-He-Believes-in-"The-Rapture" Award
Senator Mark Pryor (D-AR): When asked by Bill Maher whether he believes in evolution, Senator Pryor, a self-described evangelical, replied, "Well, I don't know. Clearly the scientific community is divided on some of the specifics of that." Pryor, who states that he believes in the Rapture, opposed repealing "Don't Ask Don't Tell" because being gay is "a sin."

Winner: The David-Vitter-Family-Values Award
Congressman Ben Quayle (R-AZ): From a Ben Quayle campaign ad: "Somebody has to go to Washington and knock the hell out of the place." More Quayle quotes from online messages he reportedly sent (note: though they sound like quotes from a drunk twenty-year-old, they're recent quotes): "That jackass was on the Dirty [a lewd Arizona gossip blog for which Quayle wrote] about 3-4 weeks ago with his little homo friend." And, "may I smell yo finger pleeeze." And, "If I was around she wouldn't ever need butt floss." Odd language for a soon-to-be candidate for Congress, but when these quotes were revealed, Quayle responded with lightning speed in an ad: "[Ben Quayle] strongly supports constitutional protection of marriage between a man and a woman." The same ad describes Quayle as being adamantly prolife and implies that unions are godless. See? Get it? If a full-grown adult, long out of college and aspiring to Congress, refers to women in bizarrely crude ways in writing, there's an ironclad defense: slam the civil rights of gay people. Also, say unions are godless. Huh? Wait. Unions are godless? I've heard people disagree with unions before—but godless? No word on any "butt floss" legislation from "family values" Quayle.

Winner: The Church-Leadership Award
Congressman Scott Rigell (R-VA): Like Michele Bachmann, Rigell graduated from Pat Robertson's Regents University. Rigell led a move to split up the Episcopal denomination because of the majority's willingness to accept gay ministers. Those are his values as an elected official as well.

Winner: The No-Back-Talk Award
Congressman Todd Rokita (R-IN): Congressman Rokita isn't satisfied with making abortion illegal in the case of rape and incest. He thinks it should be illegal even when the woman's life is in serious danger. "No exceptions." His words. Ladies, when the man says no exceptions, he means no exceptions.

Winner: The Witticisms-about-Abortion-and-Rape Award
Congressman Peter Roskam (R-IL), Chief Deputy Majority Whip: Congressman Roskam opposes a woman's right to choose without exception for rape or incest. When explaining his opposition to abortion rights for rape victims, Roskam "jokingly" asked, "Why can women have abortions if rapists cannot be executed?" Roskam proudly "led the fight against embryonic stem cell research in the [Illinois] state senate." In his legislature, Roskam led opposition to a law barring discrimination based on sexual orientation, labeling the state's Human Rights Act "a building block for gay marriage" that would "lead to some unpleasant situations."

Winner: The Jefferson-Schmefferson Award
Senator Marco Rubio (R-FL): Senator Rubio has supported allowing public schools to teach creationism. Rubio says the separation of church and state isn't in our founding documents, ignoring the fact that it was Thomas Jefferson who coined this term with reference to the First Amendment and that Jefferson, with Madison, had the greatest influence on this centrally important American principle.

Winner: The Ayn-Rand-Theocrat Award
Congressman Paul Ryan (R-WI), Budget Committee Chair: Congressman Ryan, a devotee of atheist Ayn Rand, voted against allowing embryonic stem cell research, research that could save thousands of lives. Ryan has a 100 percent voting record with the National Right to Life Committee. He voted to ban gay adoptions in Washington, DC, and to constitutionally ban gay marriage. Ryan said, "We believe, as our founders

did, that 'the pursuit of happiness' depends upon individual liberty, and individual liberty requires limited government." Oh, so that's why we need a top-down government mandate on local issues like marriage? That's why the federal government can boss around DC voters?

Winner: The One-Time-Only-Noah's-Flood Award

Congressman John Shimkus (R-IL): In an official hearing addressing concerns about rising seas because of global warming, Congressman Shimkus cited the story of Noah and the flood, saying God said that He would only destroy the earth one time. Shimkus thus implied we don't need to worry about global warming because "I do believe God's word is infallible." He also said, "There is a theological debate that this is a carbon-starved planet." Huh? Did I miss the Eleventh Thou-Shalt-Produce-Hydrocarbons Commandent?

Winner: The Big-Issues Award

Congressman Heath Shuler (D-NC): Congressman Shuler wants to make sure the word God is included in certificates with flags that fly over the Capitol. He actually put time and taxpayer money into this initiative. He also wanted to make sure that when folding flags, the eleventh fold glorifies "the God of Abraham, Isaac, and Jacob" and the twelfth fold venerates "God the Father, Son, and Holy Ghost." Meanwhile, Shuler opposes stem cell research that could save many lives and voted to allow discrimination based on sexual orientation. When in Washington, Shuler has lived at the C Street house operated by The Family.

Winner: The My-"Faith"-Means-I-Can-Discriminate-against-You-with-Your-Tax-Money Award

Congressman Lamar Smith (R-TX), Judiciary Committee Chair: Congressman Smith chairs the committee overseeing so-called faith-based initiatives. These programs take your tax money, then use it to proselytize and discriminate based on religion. Smith cosponsored a bill to eliminate abortion coverage in private insurance. Smith "asked a federal court to let him and not the Obama administration appeal a ruling that strikes down a key part of the Defense of Marriage Act," saying that he'd defend this discriminatory law more vigorously.

Winner: The As-If-Santorum-Wasn't-Enough Award

Senator Pat Toomey (R-PA): Senator Toomey supports laws permitting doctors to be thrown in jail for performing abortions and has tried to prohibit gay couples from adopting children.

Winner: The Sex-Only-in-Marriage-and-with-Prostitutes Award

Senator David Vitter (R-LA): Senator Vitter says, "Abstinence education is a public health strategy. . . . teaching teenagers that saving sex until marriage and remaining faithful afterwards is the best choice for health and happiness." The married Senator Vitter has repeatedly used the services of prostitutes (and not in some Nevada county where it's legal either). In 2003, Vitter proposed to amend our Constitution to ban same-sex marriage. In June 2006, he said, "I don't believe there's any issue that's more important than [opposing gay marriage]." In 2005, at a Lafayette Parish Republican Executive Committee lunch, Vitter compared gay marriage to hurricanes Katrina and Rita. Vitter said, "It's the crossroads where Katrina meets Rita. I always knew I was against same-sex unions." Demonstrating his Christian family values, Vitter kept Brent Furer on his taxpayer-funded payroll after Furer held his ex-girlfriend hostage, threatening to kill her with a knife. Vitter reportedly assigned Furer to help oversee women's issues for the senator's office.

Winner: The Wicked-Witch Award

Congressman Tim Walberg (R-MI): In 2008, Congressman Walberg voted "no" on funding for Head Start, because he favors religious discrimination in Head Start programs (that's illegal). Walberg warns that a Christian parochial school that takes Head Start money might have to hire—gasp— a Muslim or, love this, "a Wiccan from a coven in Ann Arbor." Walberg said, "Right now, we need to make sure that [Obama] doesn't remain as President. Whether he's American, a Muslim, a Christian, you name it."

Winner: The Basic-Life-Principles Award

Congressman Dan Webster (R-FL): Congressman Webster advocates for a group, the Institute in Basic Life Principles, which calls for "submission" by a wife and argues that a woman should not make "demands" on her husband. Webster has quoted the Rev. Tom Brandon, director of said institute, who says that it would neither be natural for a woman to work outside the home nor for a man to raise children. "That puts a wife in a role that she's not equipped for inwardly or outwardly and puts the man in the same position," Brandon says. "[The wife's] role is to trust God to supply her needs through the leadership of her husband and to serve with him and fulfill his needs." Webster says that his religious views may not always reflect his votes, but Webster has supported banning abortion with no exception for rape or incest.

Winner: The Islam-Isn't-a-Religion Award
Congressman Allen West (R-FL): Congressman West has asserted that Islam isn't a religion. West said Congressman Keith Ellison (D-MN), a Muslim, "represents the antithesis of the principles on which this country was established." (When I was a legislator, I participated in a leadership program with Ellison, who was then serving in his state legislature. Ellison struck me as a low-key guy.) West says it's "unfortunate" that gay people serve in the military and compares homosexuality to adultery.

Winner: The Other-Commandents-Are-More-Like-Guidelines Award
Congressman Lynn Westmoreland (R-GA): Congressman Westmoreland introduced legislation that would require the listing of the Ten Commandments in the House and Senate, explaining the best place for posting the commandments was not a church, but what he termed a "judicial" body. When Stephen Colbert asked Westmoreland to name the Ten Commandments, Westmoreland named only three in the broadcast (though his press secretary said his boss named seven).

Winner: The Mexican-Anchor-Zygote Award
Senator Roger Wicker (R-MS): With Congressman Duncan Hunter, Senator Wicker proposed legislation that seeks "personhood" rights for zygotes, effectively criminalizing abortion, stem cell research, common forms of birth control, and even in vitro fertilization. The once-fringe "personhood" activists were initially even renounced by fundamentalist groups. Now the extremist American Family Association, along with leading Republican politicians, embrace the personhood-for-zygotes campaign led by Les Riley, a theocrat who supports the separatist "Christian Exodus." The fun part? The personhood bill would give legal rights to the zygotes of illegal immigrants. The Manchurian zygote?

* * * * * * *

Theocratic statements may be funny at first, but when such fanatical positions are articulated by many of the 535 most powerful people in America, it makes us take stock of what a serious problem we face.

Some may say politicians are simply pandering, so we need not worry, because these politicians don't really believe their own theocratic words. Perhaps their own words, in the famous phrase of Senator Jon Kyl's office, are "not intended to be a factual statement." Certainly some just hypocritically play to the crowd, but the law is where these matters are decided. Theocratic laws harm real people whether or not those who vote for such laws are hypocrites or fanatics.

These very powerful people do not represent the values or ideals of our nation. I'm not speaking only of the days of our Founders. Just look at the mid-twentieth century. To say America was not perfect in the 1950s is a dramatic understatement. Racism was rampant. Joe McCarthy's demagoguery besmirched our nation. And yet, do yourself a favor and read Robert Caro's book, *Master of the Senate*. I've read a lot of books on American history. This one is a page turner. The dominant character—the "master" of the Senate—is Lyndon Baines Johnson. I'm not an LBJ enthusiast, but if you read this book and learn about the intellect of these legislators, not just the two savvy future presidents (Kennedy and Johnson) but also the forgotten legends (Paul Douglas, Ed Muskie, Everett Dirksen, Arthur Vandenburg, and more—Republicans and Democrats), you will see a stark contrast between them and the characters described in this chapter.

In the past, we saw brilliant and thoughtful legislators—intellectuals—whose approach to politics and policy was based on earthly reality. To be sure, there were some dolts, but overall the intellect of those lawmakers remains impressive. While rare, it is important to acknowledge Republicans like New Hampshire congressman Charlie Bass and others who seem to adhere to an older code of true libertarian Republicanism. These few Republican leaders, in the tradition of Barry Goldwater, still think theocracy shouldn't interfere with your personal life and believe that the separation of church and state is important. But there's something wrong when a society slips backward rather than moves forward, and when a body politic values rote theocracy over reasoned deliberation.

Surely there must be members of Congress today who openly profess a worldview not dominated by ancient superstition and texts, right?

7 The Secularists

I don't know that atheists should be considered as citizens, nor should they be considered patriots. This is one nation under God.

—George H. W. Bush

To discriminate against a thoroughly upright citizen because he belongs to some particular church, or because, like Abraham Lincoln, he has not avowed his allegiance to any church, is an outrage against that liberty of conscience which is one of the foundations of American life.

—Theodore Roosevelt

Winner: The Good-Ole-Fashioned-Common-Sense Award
Congressman Pete Stark (D-CA): Says Congressman Stark, "[I am a] Unitarian who does not believe in a Supreme Being. I look forward to working with the Secular Coalition to stop the promotion of narrow religious beliefs in science, marriage contracts, the military and the provision of social service." Boy, he is a very scary man! After graduating from the Massachusetts Institute of Technology, he served in the United States Air Force, then earned an MBA from the University of California, Berkeley. He next founded Security National Bank, which, in less than ten years, became a $100 million institution. Doesn't this biography just reek of radicalism? Now it's true that Pete Stark does think for himself. During the Vietnam War, most banks did not display a big peace sign outside the bank. His did. Stark was an early opponent of the Iraq invasion at a time when many Democrats supported the invasion. Stark, a veteran himself, supported reinstatement of the draft on the grounds that if America is to engage in invasions, the burden of military actions should be carried by our entire society and not "on the backs of poor people and minorities." Eighty years old on November 11, 2011, Stark has seven children and is a devoted grandparent.

We'd love to give out more secular humanist awards to members of Congress, but, umm, this chapter is basically over. That's right. The number of open nontheists in Congress today totals . . . one.

But think for a moment about all the good people who are Secular Americans and who have a made a positive contribution to our society and whose views on religion and God are essentially unreflected in Congress. Here's a quick sample of Americans living today whom you might have heard of and who have openly discussed their nontheistic views: Steve Wozniak, Seth McFarlane, Angelina Jolie, Brad Pitt, Ani DiFranco, Ira Glass, John Malkovich, Jack Nicholson, Sean Lennon, Eddie Vedder, Andy Rooney, Joss Whedon, Dave Barry, Billy Joel, George Soros, Warren Buffett, Yoko Ono, George Clooney, Bill Gates, Steven Soderbergh, Tom Wolfe, Bill Maher, Oliver Sacks, John Sayles, Michael Kinsley, James Gleick, Kevin Kline, Barbara Ehrenreich, Bill Bryson, Gabriel Byrne, Jodie Foster, Tom Lehrer, Berkeley Breathed, Jon Stewart, Randy Newman, and Penn & Teller.

Why is there only one member of Congress who openly shares a nontheistic perspective with so many other Americans? There are millions upon millions of decent honorable people who share the nontheistic views of Jodie Foster. There are far more Secular Americans than Jewish Americans. I'm perfectly happy that Jewish people, as a percentage of the population, are overrepresented in Congress. Might it not also be reasonable that there could be at least proportional representation for people who openly think like Warren Buffett, the son of a Nebraska Republican congressman? Does that sound terribly radical? Would that be unreasonable?

But for that to happen, we must build a movement with clout. That's right, clout. That's how politics works. Secular Americans must either participate fully or quit whining. The Secular Coalition for America is working now for public policy change consistent with the ideals of all Americans, religious and nonreligious, who value the separation of church and state, and in service to its coalition members.

But, if the secular movement is to grow, we must face the reality that our marketing, our strategy, our level of innovation, and our willingness to invest have generally been sleepy at best and bungled at worst. We are not reaching a broader nation. We preach primarily to our own converted. Sadly, in terms of innovation, we fall far short if we compare ourselves to religious fundamentalists, much less to Silicon Valley.

We must set our sights much higher. We should not merely match fundamentalism; we must surpass it. We must think, act, and innovate like business entrepreneurs, not sit back and expect the American people to come to us. We live in a Republic endangered by creeping theocracy. We must participate more vocally in the marketplace of ideas and reach out to a broader spectrum of our fellow citizens. I believe that now is the right time to spread our message because we have (1) demographics on our side and (2) a strategic plan imbued with the spirit of innovation. I will describe both these advantages in the next two chapters.

8 Secularism—Born Again

God will wash this nation with blood if he has to.
                                        —Glenn Beck

*I do not believe in the creed professed by the Jewish church, by the
Roman church, by the Greek church, by the Turkish church, by the
Protestant church, nor by any church that I know of. My own mind
is my own church.*

                                        —Thomas Paine

The struggle between fundamentalism (the world of Jerry Falwell, Joyce
Meyer, and Joel Osteen) on the one hand and the Jeffersonian
Enlightenment ideal on the other constitutes a central issue affecting the
future of our nation. Because America remains the most powerful and
influential nation on Earth, protecting our secular values is essential to the
future progress of civilization across the globe. If we organize, if we invest
our effort and money, and if we are willing to think strategically, I am confident of a success that will benefit America and the entire world.

As much as I respect the logistical and organizational strength of
American fundamentalism, its day is passing. As the book *American Grace*
points out, although Evangelical Protestantism, from a demographics
standpoint, grew in the 1970s and 1980s, it began to lose momentum
around 1990. Even so, its institutional and political strength remains huge
in our two-party system.

The subservience to fundamentalist ideology by the Republican Party
reached a high point with President George W. Bush—and, as evidenced by
the U.S. Congress, it risks rising higher still. Whether you are or ever were
a member of the Republican Party, it's difficult to imagine Barry Goldwater
or Gerald Ford referencing the Book of Revelations in specific connection

with military policy. President Bush did so when discussing Iraq with French president Jacques Chirac.

To have secured effective veto power over one of two major political parties in the United States represents a monumental success for religious fundamentalists. Their success has even caused Democratic politicians to feel pressure to wear their religion on their sleeves. In short, demographic stagnation notwithstanding—fundamentalist power remains as strong as it's ever been.

There are valid disagreements on economic issues between the Democratic and Republican Party. And we should not neglect the ideas espoused by the Libertarian Party, which today speaks for some traditional Republican values. But make no mistake: never before in American history have proponents of a particular religious viewpoint—and a minority viewpoint at that—secured such a potentially decisive role in our ostensibly secular Republic.

Fundamentalists have for years been fighting above their weight class. Their veto power over the Republican Party leads to the perception that the fundamentalist extremists constitute 50 percent of the American people. In fact, they represent about 24 percent of Americans at most. This bootstrapping of political influence has certainly affected politics and perception, but it has also affected policy. The political realities today are profoundly different from those of 1960, when secular policy was largely a matter of consensus. Jack Kennedy was almost uniformly applauded for his speech in Houston favoring church-state separation, and Richard Nixon avoided direct criticism of Kennedy's speech for fear of a backlash (though his fundamentalist allies spoke ill of Kennedy's speech). One can only imagine the litany of pejoratives that the Republican Party would throw at that speech if delivered today. Indeed, Senator Rick Santorum and former governor Sarah Palin have both reached back five decades to condemn Kennedy's Houston speech.

Theocratic laws permeate our statute books. The Republican Party, by any measure, is strong, not weak. They are extremely well funded and well organized. Someday the Republican Party may return to the more libertarian roots of a Barry Goldwater. That is, however, not happening soon, especially not without a counterforce.

Secular Americans must work so that our political clout matches our numbers. Data vary, but look at the percentage of Americans from a recent poll who take a science-based view of the world or do not affiliate with a religion, by age group:

- 7 percent of those 65 and over

- 13 percent of those ages 50–64

- 18 percent of those ages 30–49

- 25 percent of those under 30

As a whole, the "nones" (people who report no religious affiliation) shot up dramatically from 7 percent of Americans in 1990 to 17 percent today. Considering the number of secular Jews, secular Catholics, and secular liberal Protestants who may for cultural reasons identify themselves by their religious heritage, it's clear that the number of Americans who care about secular values is vastly undercounted.

This underreporting is not the result of some conspiracy, but the result of polling questions that are just not phrased to get the most accurate result. To some degree, Secular Americans also face an almost unconscious cultural bias, including from people who bear Secular Americans no ill will or who may even be Secular Americans themselves.

To collect better data, better polling questions are necessary. For example, assume you've agreed to participate in a poll and are asked this series of questions:

1. Do you think fundamentalist Christians have too much influence in America today?

2. Do you tend to agree or disagree with those who think the government should restrict choices about one's sexual life based on their interpretation of the Bible?

3. Do you believe Zodiac signs can in fact predict personality traits or predict the future? Or do you think they are just for fun?

4. Do you value scientific reasoning over supernatural explanations for the world around us?

5. Do you think the Earth was created a few thousand years ago as told in the Bible or do you believe that the Earth is billions of years old as scientists conclude?

6. Do you think that one must accept Christ as one's personal savior in order to have eternal life?

7. Do you think that a child born in Hindu culture who dies without having accepted Christ will go to hell?

8. Do you accept the conclusion of scientists that human beings evolved over hundreds of thousands of years? Or do you believe that humans were created as told in the Bible?

9. Do you believe the creation stories of the Druids? Or the creation stories of Australian Aborigines? Do you believe in the creation stories of any non-Judeo-Christian religions?

10. Do you believe that Jesus in fact rose from the dead?

11. Do you believe that Jesus was in fact born of a virgin?

12. Are you uncertain about whether there is life after death?

13. Do you have doubts about whether hell exists?

14. Do you have doubts about whether heaven exists?

15. Do you believe that if someone prays for rain, it will increase the likelihood of rain?

16. Do you tend to believe that if someone prays to live longer or prays to ward off disease, a God will intervene on behalf of that one person and not on behalf of others who do not pray?

17. Do you sometimes question, if only to yourself, whether there is a God?

18. Do you have a question in your mind about the morality of an all-powerful God that could allow 9/11, the Haiti disaster, the Kennedy assassination, the Japanese tsunami, the Tucson shooting, and the Holocaust?

19. Do you think there is an actual devil?

20. Do you think that a God makes decisions about what will happen to you personally?

These questions are mere examples. Many expressly religious people would no doubt agree with a nontheist's answers to several of these questions. This series of questions gives the person answering time—time to think about what they really think.

There is no doubt that millions upon millions of Americans strongly assert their belief that the Bible is literally true. Indeed, far more Americans assert this than do citizens of most any other nation—thus, our challenge. And yet, many Americans, if they took their time with questions like those posed here, would feel comfortable answering that, yes, really, in their heart of hearts, they are uncertain about the existence of God, of life after death, of heaven, and of the efficacy of prayer.

At a minimum, this would make them agnostic—meaning they claim no certainty about God's existence or matters such as Christ's actual divinity. And many, if they honestly thought about such questions, might even say that they lack belief in a god or gods. I can't say what that percentage of the population might be. But I'll guarantee you this: that percentage is far, far higher than the number of people who will say flat-out yes to the following question, which almost shouts off the page:

ARE YOU NOW OR HAVE YOU EVER BEEN AN ATHEIST?

Yes, of course, none of the polls ever use the McCarthy-era phrase, "Are you now or have you ever been…?" Yet the word "atheist" is loaded with dark historical connotations related to the era of "godless" Communism. Speaking as a happy capitalist myself—and a lifelong believer in the scientific method—there is something about the word atheist that calls to mind Joseph Stalin. And darn it, I don't like Joe Stalin! I don't like his moustache, I don't like his economics, I don't like that he killed millions of people. I want nothing—zero—to do with that guy. Many people blanch at the word atheist because of these associations. (In truth, Stalin created what amounted to his own religion and was treated, by his own design, as a form of deity that is always watching. Stalin even had the secret police at his disposal to make the "always watching" possibility monstrously credible.)

So the word atheist is laden with cultural and historical connotations, rendering the word jarring to most people despite the fact that all these connotations have little to do with the simple definition of the word. Also, there's a perception, perhaps in certain instances justified, that some activist atheists seek to attack people as stupid rather than to criticize policies and ideas as harmful.

The word itself is unrelated to all these perceptions. Brad Pitt is an atheist because he happens to not believe in a god or gods. This does not diminish in any way all the charitable work he does. Indeed, because Pitt focuses on helping people in the here and now, Pitt's worldview may enhance his proven charitable ethic. Also, the label "atheist" and the seemingly more cuddly label "agnostic" need not be mutually exclusive. An agnostic atheist would simply be someone who lacks belief in a god or gods but who also claims no certainty informing their lack of belief.

In our quick focus on labels, though, what's most important is often forgotten: respect and caring for people as people. My parents divorced when I was little, so I had the benefit of two mothers. My stepmom, Marilyn, came from a fundamentalist background, accepted and welcomed people of all stripes, and treated them with kindness and respect. And she treated me as her own son from day one. Agree or disagree with the church of her youth, time and again she taught me to be kindhearted and accepting of other people. I've always called her mom and she set an admirable example.

Sometimes I'm not sure Secular Americans follow that welcoming approach as well as we should. Even if you disagree with someone, you can joke, talk, be friends, and have a beer with them—and, most importantly, avoid personal vitriol. And, if you want to persuade someone, build that personal connection before whacking them over the head with our oh-so-important issues. My mom's example can be valuable, indeed ennobling. If we take this approach, and remain consciously positive and helpful like my mom, maybe the perception of words like atheist will change.

Despite the often unfair stereotypes, the number of Secular Americans, according to all measures, is on the rise, particularly among the young. My focus is on policy not on labels, and I think the term agnostic is entirely comfortable and welcoming to many people. Although agnostics sometimes get no respect from theists and atheists alike, the good-old agnostic is simply saying that, with no absolute proof, I'm going to make no assumptions. More importantly, they are Secular Americans—people who, in their daily lives, expect nothing supernatural will intervene for or against them. It's all up to us. It's called personal responsibility.

Some might argue (okay, I might argue) that Eleanor Roosevelt was the greatest woman in the history of the world, and certainly a person widely and justifiably admired. Far more Americans than are currently counted in any poll as agnostic will agree with Eleanor Roosevelt when she said, "I don't know whether I believe in a future life." She went on to say, "You have to accept whatever comes, and the only thing is that you meet it with courage and with the best that you have to give."

Once we get behind the facades and the wish not to offend, there are legions of patriotic, good Americans who think just as Eleanor Roosevelt did regarding life's ultimate questions. Whether they embrace the label or not, these many millions are Secular Americans. They make decisions based on the realities of our world. From the perspective of Americans who think like Eleanor Roosevelt, the possibility that there's some supernatural being somewhere running the show is not relevant to how they live their lives day by day.

Many religious labels are more cultural than a reflection of theology. There are millions of Americans, most of whom would never label themselves atheist—indeed, who might well label themselves Catholic or Jewish or Protestant or Muslim—who, as a practical matter, think an Abrahamic God intervening in our daily lives is as likely to be true as the myth of Thor—that is, they think the odds are vanishingly close to nil.

Those who do the analyzing, even when they are of good will, are sometimes implicitly biased against Secular Americans. For example, the book *American Grace* provides a valuable survey of America's diverse religious landscape since the mid-twentieth century. Yet the authors, at one point, refer to the "nones" (people who don't affiliate with a religion) as "extreme." They contrast the "nones" with old-line Protestantism and Catholicism, labeling those denominations moderate. If you ask most people, they will label themselves as moderate ("It's that other guy who's extreme!"). And, thus, if something is labeled as extreme, then people tend to shy away from whatever is so labeled.

I fully accept that the term "extreme" should be used when warranted by evidence, but, say what you will, Bill Gates and Warren Buffet are anything but extreme. These brilliant business leaders lack a God belief. Yet, they are thoughtful, charitable, and quintessentially moderate. The only thing extreme about them is that extreme smarts and extreme hard work led them to becoming extremely successful. Their moral values are as mainstream and American as apple pie.

The idea that people who take a scientific world view and have no God belief are "extreme"—or, to quote Lennon, "carryin' pictures of Chairman Mao"—is a baseless stereotype. This notion is completely unrelated to what modern Secular Americans think.

As a politician in Maine, I earned support the old-fashioned way by visiting my neighbors and campaigning door to door—thousands upon thousands of doors. Through direct observation I saw that, except among fundamentalists, church attendance decreased significantly over my decade in office. My fellow Bangor residents were good people who cared about our local schools and about local charities. These very people, when I campaigned on Sunday morning, were increasingly cultivating their gardens, spending time with their families—and not going to church.

I observed this trend through another lens as well. Notwithstanding my opinions regarding some church policies, I love churches, and I admire the beauty of Bangor's lovely St. John's Catholic Church. (I love synagogues too and, though I've not spent much time in mosques, I'm sure I'd find them just as fascinating). My love for religious architecture stemmed in part from a course I took at Notre Dame, in which the professor instilled an appreciation of the creativity and craft that went into building the great cathedrals of centuries past. It also stemmed from a wonderful book titled *Pillars of the Earth*. What greater opportunity was there in 1400 to contribute to something of timeless beauty and collaborative will? I know—"They built those European cathedrals on the backs of peasants." Fair point, but the beauty stands. In Maine, low-income Catholics willingly contributed to the building of St. John's. And yet, I could see that religious services were becoming almost archaic, something one might tip a hat to at Christmas, Easter, or Passover out of respect for older relatives, but not really something that was truly part of one's daily life—and this trend made the people of Bangor no less honest or caring.

As the data makes clear, young people are increasingly secular, and they are as bright and idealistic as any generation I've seen, but they have taken the example of their parents' generation even more to heart and are attending religious services even less frequently than their parents did. Even with the underreporting of Secular Americans, the growth of secularism is dramatic. This growth will continue with each passing generation. To paraphrase Mick Jagger, time is on our side. Secular America is on the rise. We must now press our advantage strategically. If we simply gloat about growing demographics, we will fail.

If we pursue an intelligent strategic plan, we will succeed, and America will flourish as it was designed—as a secular, constitutional Republic—as a nation that offers protections and benefits to both those who believe in the inerrancy of ancient texts and those who embrace Enlightenment values.

9 Our Secular Decade

A Strategic Plan

I think it's time for us to just hand it over to God and say, "God, You're going to have to fix this."... I think it's time for us to use our wisdom and our influence and really put it in God's hands. That's what I'm going to do, and I hope you'll join me.

—Rick Perry

The great decisions of government cannot be dictated by the concerns of religious factions.... We have succeeded for 205 years in keeping the affairs of state separate from the uncompromising idealism of religious groups and we mustn't stop now. To retreat from that separation would violate the principles of conservatism and the values upon which the framers built this democratic republic.

—Barry Goldwater

If you're like me, you've often heard a particular Margaret Mead quote from friends on the Left, or at least noticed it on a poster taped to the office wall of a liberal nonprofit: "Never doubt that a small group of committed people can change the world. Indeed, it is the only thing that ever has." And yet, if there's one group to whom this quote very aptly applies, it's the so-called Religious Right. In the late 1960s they looked at America, and the fundamentalists did not like what they saw: women defying the roles mandated by the Bible; gay activists rearing their "perverted" heads to fight for rights in violation of biblical law; and civil rights groups successfully fighting against biblically "commanded" segregation.

From the perspective of fundamentalists, the social justice preaching of a Martin Luther King or a Robert Kennedy flew in the face of their most essential values—a perspective vociferously echoed by Glenn Beck in recent times. As fate would have it, King and Kennedy were struck down. Some might say it was God's will. (My father remembers to this day a man across the street from the house where I grew up in Orange County, California, who said to my dad of Robert Kennedy, "I hope that son of a bitch gets shot like his brother.") Regardless, if Robert Kennedy had lived to secure his party's nomination, the polls showed him defeating Nixon in a walk. That wasn't a risk fundamentalists could take again. And so a small group of committed people, people at the time considered little more than an antiquated and rejected relic of the 1925 Scopes Trial, rose faster and stronger than any phoenix and transformed America in their own image.

Forget about posters taped to the wall at your local nonprofit. The fundamentalists got the job done. So much so that, as the megachurches grew and grew, the politicians listened and listened like never before.

In August 1980 presidential candidate Ronald Reagan gave his historically pivotal speech to a vast crowd of fundamentalist ministers in Dallas, Texas, in which he sought to tear down a wall—the wall separating church and state. Knowing that religious organizations are not supposed to engage in political endorsements, Reagan made a statement that continues to echo to this day: "I know that you can't endorse me, but . . . I want you to know I endorse you and what you are doing." The Republican Party, with that speech, crossed a theocratic Rubicon and has never looked back.

As a politician, I know when to tip my hat to my competitors, and I tip my hat to the fundamentalists. I give the theocrats their deserved due. It's the only sportsmanlike response.

As executive director of Secular Coalition for America, an organization of which few Americans have ever heard, I intend to see them and raise them. Why be alive if you don't want a challenge?

America is the greatest nation on earth—because of our constitutional ideals and our founding principles. It's time for Secular Americans to earn our nation's respect, admiration, and understanding. It's time for America to know that secularists seek not to attack and disdain our country, but rather to serve our nation at this critical juncture. The struggle of gay people for civil rights has contributed greatly to America's journey toward meeting its best ideals. Gay-rights activists started small and grew unexpectedly powerful. Today Secular Americans are the right people at the right to time to take a leadership role in America's next great step forward. Secular Americans can, and will, play a prominent role in leading America back to its highest shared ideals: freedom, reason, equality, justice, compassion, and passion.

The fundamentalists made their voices heard. How do we secularists do even better? Here's how:

Our Secular Decade: A Patriotic Plan to Reclaim America
Increased advocacy on public policy issues must drive our entire strategy. Successful advocacy isn't only about citing statistics or promoting statutes. Our success requires sharing and communicating stories—stories that vividly demonstrate the adverse and real effects of religious privileging in public policy.

Consider Lincoln's Gettysburg address. 256 words. What Lincoln did was tell a story of our people and our country—concisely and powerfully.

Jack Kennedy sent a man to the moon. He didn't lead with statistics and statutes. He inspired with a story. He told the story of boys traveling across the Irish countryside. When they came to an orchard wall that was too high and too difficult to permit their voyage to continue, they took off their caps—and tossed them over the wall—and then they had no choice but to follow them. America's best scientists were not at all certain how to technically achieve Kennedy's dramatic goal, especially not within ten years. But it was the drama, excitement, and specificity of Kennedy's passionate, inspiring vision and clear goal that inspired relentless work and innovation.

Now, as Gerald Ford said, I'm no Lincoln. And as Lloyd Bentsen said to Dan Quayle, I'm no Jack Kennedy. But since 2009, I've been listening and learning, reading, then listening more. In crafting a strategy that will bring secular success, I've been listening carefully to Secular Americans and to the mood of all Americans. From that listening, I find that we must better illustrate in our public discourse the real experiences of Americans. Our central public policy strategy must be to tell stories of how our fellow citizens—real people—are harmed by the privileging of religion in law.

Stories of religious bias in law not only outrage and unite active secularists, but they also attract new people who might otherwise not have thought about the importance of secular issues. They can be attracted if we tell them simple and compelling stories that express these very real injustices taking place in the United States.

Secularists revere reason and an evidence-based approach as the highest and best standard for leading a good and positive life. This is what I've described as a noble flaw. Children prefer stories to a recitation of facts to be engaged and energized. Adults are no different. Secularists sometimes dismiss stories as mere "anecdotal evidence." Wrong. A tendency toward relying on high-flown abstraction sometimes undermines our best intentions and the prospect of achieving our highest principles. Stories illustrate a larger point, sustained and supported by statistics and a careful review of statutes. Stories offer a lens through which to understand the experiences of individuals and illustrate the larger impact of policy decisions on our communities. Without stories, our cause is lost.

The old activist methods—focusing on a religious national motto or the Pledge, or mangers in a town square or crosses on public land—indeed employ valid legal arguments, but they do not pulse with the flesh and blood necessary to move a larger audience.

As seen throughout this book, we face numerous examples, particularly from recent decades, of laws that are based not on equal treatment but outright religious bias—laws that harm our fellow citizens. In extreme cases, the unjust bias in law plays a role in the physical harm of our fellow citizens, sometimes even the death of children.

We must unite around the idea that our fellow human beings should not be harmed—nor hoodwinked—by religious bias in law.

This unifying cause, expressed in human terms, is one that can garner support and participation from millions of Americans who find the rise of theocratic politics in America repugnant, but who have yet to find an organized outlet for their concerns. Our strategy for growth will be built on this idea and executed through a series of well-defined objectives.

Secular Decade Strategic Objectives
Objective: Increase advocacy by telling more stories and telling them better. The Secular Coalition for America Web site (www.secular.org) is an effective tool for communicating stories and spreading our message. You can post videos from our Web site on Facebook, mention them to your friends or colleagues over drinks or dinner, "tweet" about them. Maybe you can persuade a friendly but skeptical coworker—or your in-laws—of the harm caused to real people by religious bias in law if you offer specific examples. You can direct friends to our Web site or direct friends to this book. The stories that we share on our site, and the videos that go with them, have a simple purpose: to demonstrate to friends, family, and neighbors that secularism enhances a moral vision for America's future by redressing concrete harm to real people.

Objective: Increase advocacy with a greater lobbying presence. There was no such thing as a secular lobbyist as recently as 2005. I'm so proud to be an advocate—a lobbyist—for secularism because, time and again, issue after issue, our secular policies call for compassion, justice, and inclusion. In times of overheated rhetoric, when God is frequently invoked to judge, to condemn, to ostracize, to discriminate, America needs the compassionate voice of secularism. We display our deep moral values through our actions on behalf of our fellow human beings, not by our willingness to condemn our fellow human beings.

Don't think so? Think about the inclusive nature of our lobbying goals versus the discriminatory lobbying goals of fundamentalists, such as the Focus on the Family crowd. After ten years in politics, two years as legal counsel to my state senate, and two years lobbying for my state bar association, I have strong opinions about lobbying strategy. My job as Majority Whip of my legislature was to count votes and, when necessary, lobby my party colleagues. Knowing the issues inside and out is critical, but understanding the elected official (and his or her staff) can be dispositive. However, a big part of my job is strategic planning and public speaking, so we are lucky to have a full-time lobbyist working for secularism in Washington, DC. We need more soon. One is not enough. By 2020 we must have multiple full-time lobbyists fighting against theocratic policies.

Objective: Increase advocacy by strengthening our media message. Proud as I am of our lobbying for justice, Secular Coalition for America must have a clear message that connects to a broader audience than Congress itself. We must have the people to spread that message.

Whatever else you say about him, Ronald Reagan offered a consistent message. Consistency is effective. The statement, backed by evidence, that religious bias in law harms real people will be our urgent, constant drumbeat. Those who attack religion as an abstract concept often have entirely valid arguments; however, our strategy, consciously designed to appeal to many millions of our fellow citizens, should demonstrate the appeal of secular values by tugging at heartstrings and illustrating specific injustices in law that harm our fellow human beings.

We are tribunes of justice for the vulnerable—not attackers. Our cause will grow as a result of this consistent tactic—and consistent message, which must be communicated strongly, relentlessly, and widely in a way that penetrates the consciousness of the mainstream media.

Objective: Broaden our base of supporters by establishing a Secular Coalition for America affiliate in every state by 2020. In 2020 you will see fifty statewide Secular Coalition for America affiliates. Because we evidence-based secularists believe that people who live in Washington, DC, are, in fact, human beings, we will actually aim to have fifty-one affiliates. Participants will be identified by congressional district in each state. Secular Coalition for America will train volunteers to organize congressional office visits and to convey ourselves as the polite, articulate people we are. When I was in politics I responded to the magic words, "I am your constituent and I really need your help."

State affiliate volunteers can use the issues listed on the Secular Coalition for America Web site as an easy template for federal issues when they go to meet with their local congressperson and congressional staffers. Consistent with our mission, they will organize to speak out to their state legislature as well.

Secular Coalition for America will continue to build its electronic presence, but when Secular Americans—millions of Secular Americans—have a grass roots and in-person outlet for their idealism and for their passions on issues, we will witness a dramatic effect. The hard crunch of grassroots organizing is something I care deeply about and an area where secularism has been weak.

I once considered running for a legislative seat in a very Republican year, when legislatures across America went strongly Republican. I made at the time what seemed to be a foolhardy decision. What decision? Well . . . Stephen King was the richest guy in Bangor. The folks who owned the local oil company were a close second. The next richest guy owned the local landfill. My foolhardy decision was running for public office in a bad year for Democrats against the third richest guy in town. In fact, my opponent's roots in Maine stretched back to the 1800s. He paid for the local ice-skating rink—a justifiably big deal in Maine for which he earned deserved thanks. He served on the board of multiple organizations in town. An affable man, he had given generously to our community. I was tagged as a liberal lawyer from Southern California who'd lived in Bangor six years. My opponent had "means" and he spent those funds unhesitatingly. I was broke as usual. I knocked on Stephen King's door. Stephen King gave me a thousand bucks and voted for me. That was exciting. And I won—which was even more exciting.

But I didn't win because of Stephen King. I won because I decided to knock on his door, then the door of a guy in a trailer park—and then continued to knock on hundreds of more doors in trailer parks. I was told poor people in trailer parks don't vote (kind of like I'm now told that Secular Americans are a silent, nonparticipating bunch). But I listened to what people faced in Maine. I was willing to act upon their concerns. Similarly, our ears must remain open to listen for injustice in law based on religious privileging. We will change the world because Secular Coalition for America is now listening nationwide. And our ability to send information to the grass roots and gather information from the grass roots will increase exponentially. We will tell stories that relate the injustice of putting dogma over people, and we will bring our ever-compassionate secular message wherever we go.

Secular Coalition for America's fifty-state plan is both the single most important step we must take to be an effective lobbying group, and the single most important step we can take to increase the membership of our ten member organizations and our entire secular movement.

Why?

First, in order to increase our clout in Washington, we must increase our clout back home. E-mail and social media efforts are very effective and meaningful, but they must be complemented by people—articulate, passionate, local people—ready to speak out from their home turf and tell their stories to elected officials and their staff in person.

Second, we must strengthen the infrastructure of the secular movement. The percentage of Secular Americans who are involved as activists is small. The existence of state Secular Coalitions will help grow our movement. The Coalition's affiliate agreement specifically requires that state Secular Coalition for America groups must contact and offer inclusion to our member organizations' local affiliates within their state. This will allow Secular Coalition for America and its member organizations to grow and to work together to increase the secular movement's activist base.

You can help establish a Secular Coalition for your home state. It is the single most important step in building our success. Take action now by going to our Web site www.secular.org and reviewing the template affiliate agreement. Well-organized volunteers are the primary leaders of our state affiliates. That could be you.

Objective: Broaden our base of supporters through improved social networking. We must communicate not only with our base but also with the many more who might join and grow our base. We must also connect average people harmed by religious bias in law and we must have an Internet team poised and ready to react to injustice—then energize our compassionate audience with those stories. Our e-mail list, Facebook friends, blog readers, and Twitter followers are increasing. We plan to invest more time and resources to promote and advance our cause through social networks, more sophisticated search-engine optimization, and online advertising. But all those techniques are simply that: techniques. I picture a young person in a small fundamentalist town who loves Voltaire, Whitman, Jefferson,

Darrow, Einstein, and Darwin. I want that young person to know their values have a public-policy home. I want that small-town person to feel at home with Secular Coalition for America and our public-policy mission.

Objective: Broaden our base of supporters through outreach to the "unconverted." Many millions of Americans actually share our secular values, but the vast majority of Americans are unaware that there exists an organized voice to represent those values. I know this because, until I got this job, I didn't know there was an organization that represented my moral values. Secular Coalition for America has many potential allies, including

- the science and technology community
- the LGBT community
- libertarians
- women's rights organizations
- peace and justice groups
- civil-liberties advocates
- average Secular Americans in need of a home for their policy views

Secular American activism must expand. Well before 2020, Secular Coalition for America must be able to communicate electronically with a supporter list that is at least six-figures strong—so that Capitol Hill will have no choice but to pay attention.

Our outreach staff is essential to what we do. We must hire more dedicated outreach staff. Increased numbers of people means increased clout.

One example: You may disagree with certain aspects of the true libertarian perspective, but true libertarians do not want Big Brother deciding our personal lives on behalf of anyone's interpretation of the Bible. Many theocrats now in Congress parade as "libertarians," but they are only playing dress-up (Ron Paul and Rand Paul, for example). Americans may disagree about economic policy, but when it comes to the government staying out of our personal lives, the great majority is a libertarian majority. True libertarians have a passionate following. Secular Coalition for America will tap that idealism and that of the numerous other demographics I've listed that share our ideals.

Objective: Become full participants in elective politics. Many get upset about political preaching from the pulpit, a violation of law for a tax-deductible religion. But what about the political speech from fundamentalist extremists that is perfectly legal? They spend millions on political action, including through 501(c)(4)s. Under Citizens United, 501(c)(4) corporations can spend money on political advocacy. By contrast, Secular Americans are often as silent as the grave when it comes to political giving. This must change.

Secular Americans must take a sophisticated approach to electioneering and campaign contributions. We will become a significant force by 2020. In 1972, the "mainstream" deemed gay people as little more than perverts to be shunned. Hard work—and major giving—changed the perception and thus the reality. You may have heard this rumor: politicians want money. We will craft a separate and targeted investment strategy in electioneering. Our absolutely nonpartisan approach at Secular Coalition for America will support the true advocates—Democrat, Republican, or Libertarian—who cast votes for separation of church and state. We must fully participate in the process if we expect to influence the process. To be blunt: that has not even been close to happening. This will change.

Objective: See ten openly secular elected officials in Congress by 2020. As a state legislator in Maine, I represented all the people of my town, but I increasingly saw that, while the fundamentalist extremists were quite vocal in the halls of my legislature (and fundamentalist extremists were even more vocal in other states), my views—my secular views—were actually more in sync with the citizens I represented. Reading Susan Jacoby's book *Freethinkers* was when I realized there is a deep heritage to my values as a Secular American. I know that there are more members of Congress than Pete Stark who share those values. Maybe they are from a district in which it's tough to win reelection. Having served as Majority Whip, I would fully understand a politician representing some rural part of Texas who kept his agnosticism to himself.

However, I'm confident that members of Congress in other districts could, without significant political damage, acknowledge the proud values and tradition that they represent: the values of Walt Whitman, the values of Thomas Paine, the values of the young Lincoln. If we can get ten of them to openly say so by 2020, our nation's vision will be more clear.

America already knows that Angelina Jolie and Brad Pitt are good and decent Americans. Americans rightly admire Jolie's work in Africa. Pitt returns again and again to New Orleans, years after the flood, to make a positive difference. They represent something very good about America. Openly nontheist members of Congress can do something very meaningful as well, simply by setting an example. You know who you are. We already know of over twenty-five secular members of Congress in office today, and those are just the ones who have said so to us confidentially.

In the meantime, Secular Coalition for America will also support and honor openly secular officials elected at the local and state level. For example, Kyrsten Sinema, a dynamic, articulate, state senator in Arizona, was named by *Time* magazine as one of forty elected officials under forty who are up-and-comers. I don't know if State Senator Sinema will be president or a U.S. senator one day, but Senator Sinema spoke at the kick-off of Secular Coalition for Arizona, and this smart, dynamic secular elected official has great potential to be a national figure, and already has major accomplishments.

We also intend to help candidates that speak out for our issues, regardless of their personal religious views. We intend to highlight and praise them, wherever they come from in the United States. This combined cultivation of current and up-and-coming politicians will lead to better and more accurate representation of the American tapestry. Until we secure our fair share of representation, Congress does not represent America fully.

I remember being told on numerous occasions that it was politically impossible for a black person to be elected president in my lifetime. I said, yes, it's possible—with a top-quality candidate. I can walk to the White House from my office in less than ten minutes, and there is now an African-American who has a pretty decent office in that building from what I hear. African-Americans represent a smaller percentage of American society (approximately 13 percent) than those who identify with no religion (approximately 15 percent). The experiences and beliefs of African-Americans are not uniform. The experiences and beliefs of Secular Americans are not uniform. Both groups have enriched this country tremendously and have made, and will continue to make, important contributions to our country.

Bear in mind that Secular Coalition for America does an election report card on candidates. If a devout Catholic like a Kennedy or a born-again Christian (have you heard the statements Jimmy Carter's been making in recent years?) supports our issues, then we support them. Absolutely. I've never been a big fan of what is known as identity politics (politicians who do a good job should be thanked regardless of background). That said, the diversity of America warrants diverse representation. Something is wrong if a group of many millions lacks significant congressional representation.

Objective: Strengthen bonds within our Coalition. Secular Coalition for America represents a unique, ever-strengthening conglomeration of organizations with a diverse variety of philosophies. In fact, when considering that two of our member organizations are nontheistic religions, you start to grasp the impressive challenge that our founding board president Herb Silverman and many others overcame to even create our Coalition. The history within the secular movement includes some degree of infighting and division. Secular Coalition for America embodies the vision, desire, and ability to overcome that flaw of the past by pointing to and focusing on our collective, shared mission with idealistic and pragmatic passion.

Our founding philosophy of unity and our strategic plan seek to more effectively knit together Secular Coalition for America's member groups through improved communication and a common vision for the future. We will improve the professional abilities of our still too small but growing staff to become more sophisticated servants of our Coalition, and we will conduct surveys that cultivate ideas and inspiration from our member groups.

The biggest step for our Coalition? We must face the mental challenge that, while overcoming infighting within the Coalition is wonderful, the stark reality remains that our Coalition in aggregate is too small. If you don't believe it, examine the budget of Focus on the Family and the many other fundamentalist organizations that influence Washington so effectively. Focus on the Family, one important group of many fundamentalist policy organizations, has an annual budget north of $120 million. Our focus therefore must be outward not inward and we must focus on collective growth and appeal to a wider demographic. This strategic plan is designed to serve that larger mission.

Objective: Build a culture of innovation and growth within the Coalition. I mentioned that in Bangor I saw mainline Protestantism dying off, Roman Catholicism losing momentum, and synagogue attendance going down as well. Despite much of my social life revolving around at least nominal members of these religions, their community presence sometimes seemed a little dusty, a little musty, and less dynamic than the fundamentalist churches. Fundamentalists tended to be energized, energizing, and clean-cut. Perhaps more importantly, they market that clean-cut energetic style. If they can have that success for fundamentalist extremism, we can have that success for secularism and justice.

Pastorpreneur is a well-known book among fundamentalists. I admire the concept of "pastorpreneurship." Fundamentalist Christians take a business approach to marketing and growing their community. This approach largely began in the 1970s and has continued to develop. Rick Warren is an impressive practitioner of this approach. His business strategy has made him very wealthy (as we know, with the help of unjust tax loopholes). But there's no discounting his success, nor similar successes among fundamentalists in every corner of America.

In contrast, among secularists, the tone sometimes seems a bit . . . retrograde. Attend one of our conventions and witness the many arcane debates about the names to call ourselves; the arcane debates about how to counter creationism, or intelligent design (or whatever the latest marketing name is for biblical creation myths); the discussions of how offensive it is that the postal service printed a Mother Teresa stamp, or that "In God We Trust" is engraved on coins. Don't get me wrong: I long ago concluded that Darwin was right, and it takes an eighth-grade history class to know that religious symbols on public land is the result of politics, not strict adherence to our Constitution. That said, none of these ideas—none of these symbolic issues—constitute a sufficient marketing tactic necessary to appeal to, and to attract, the broader general public.

Moreover, despite the clear evidence that Secular Americans tend to be younger Americans, older people generally dominate the leadership of our movement. Ageism is wrong in either direction. Older people have much to offer, but we must also include the young professionals and innovators from all fields if we are to succeed. Secular Coalition for America takes an entrepreneurial approach, seeking to spread that approach to our entire movement.

Objective: Regularly schedule secular strategic summits. As executive director of Secular Coalition for America, I am proud of our strategic plan so far, but I know that it's not good enough. I want bold new leaders to say, "Thanks! It's time to do more and to do it better. Here's how." To that end, in May 2011 we held our first biennial strategic summit to allow new faces with bold ideas to come to the forefront. It was a big success and you can see a video of the summit at www.secular.org.

Our biennial summit isn't a conference where people sit and listen to lectures. It's where our best and brightest participate fully in improving the strategic plan I am presenting to you now. They do so in conjunction with the leadership of our ten coalition organizations. In turn, perhaps our coalition leaders say to themselves, that person is smart, I want them on our board. We must bring in new minds and ideas.

This summit strategizes every two years. We draw together bold leaders with specific pragmatic ideas for our future. To avoid bringing lawsuits willy-nilly, the summit also brings together lawyers so that we might take a more strategic approach to secular litigation, act in concert, and connect legal efforts with our lobbying efforts. One such possibility involves greater selectivity in picking where and when to make a legal move.

The summit brings mainstream media, marketing, and social media professionals together to discuss success in marketing our approach to a secular government. The summit holds a lobby day to get Secular Americans onto Capitol Hill to advocate to Congress. Most importantly, summit participants help produce ideas and develop specific tactics for all the objectives of our Secular Decade strategic plan.

Objective: Commit to continuous strategic planning and innovation. While the strategic summit occurs once every two years, the Secular Decade plan will evolve, grow, and become more detailed with continuous revision and participation. The beauty of an evidence-based approach to life is the willingness—the flexibility—to adjust and to change based on new information. That is how this strategic plan will move forward. We have a strategic group within the Coalition continually monitoring our progress.

Objective: Offer high-quality internships. Remember Sarah Palin dismissing community organizers? Secular Coalition for America provides a place where secular community organizers are cultivated and trained—and gain valuable experience.

Our internship program for young people serves not just Secular Coalition for America but the entire movement and mission. We are bringing young people to Washington to make a difference. We have applicants from all over wanting to make a difference on behalf of the values of Jefferson and Madison. Some of the alumni of this effort will be secular elected officials in years to come.

Objective: Broaden and deepen our financial base. We must raise money like any organization, and in 2010 I introduced different donor societies on our Web site. I like them because they build a sense of community and investment, and one of the perks of my job was to pick the names of our societies. Our society names have a sentimental meaning for me. We Secular Americans are not united by disbelief but by a deeply held belief. Our belief is embodied in the actions and life stories of Americans who made a big and positive difference in our country—and for whom the Coalition's donor societies are named.

For example, Thomas Paine, the Father of the American Revolution, said, "My religion is to do good." That quote is on my business card, not because I've necessarily gotten all that much done, but because I want to remind myself of the goal every time I look in my wallet. Elizabeth Cady Stanton said, "The Bible and the Church have been the greatest stumbling blocks in the way of women's emancipation."

These individuals, along with Twain and Darrow, Jefferson and Madison, and genius immigrants Lennon and Einstein, represent the best we have to offer as a species. And thus when people give to Secular Coalition for America, they give in the name of our heroes. These non-mythological beings inspire us to move forward and, with all their flaws, are the best guide to our future improvement as a citizenry. They inspire our continuously evolving strategic plan—a plan that will only improve with your active participation.

What You Can Do

Because Secular Coalition for America is in the first of many decades, your active help now is not a drop in the bucket. You can carve out a place for yourself as an early leader in our historic effort in the following ways:

1. Help organize a Secular Coalition affiliate for your state. A template agreement and start-up kit is on our Web site, www.secular.org.

2. Sign up for our e-mails on our Web site, post our videos to Facebook and e-mail them to family and friends, and urge family and friends to sign up for our action alerts.

3. Give money to one or more of our ten member organizations and to Secular Coalition for America, and ask family and friends to join you in doing so.

4. Encourage your family and friends to read this book and participate in the Secular Decade plan. Twitter about this book. Post about it on Facebook.

5. Support those candidates who support the separation of church and state.

6. Run for your local city council, your local school board, or your state legislature.

When we exercise secular leadership—by running for office, by donating money, by organizing a state Secular Coalition, by using our social media skills—we are making our own contribution to the tradition of Paine, Stanton, Twain, Darrow, and Lennon. We are helping to build an American future worthy of our past.

10 A Vision of a Secular America

Within the covers of the Bible are all the answers for all the problems men face.
                                                    —Ronald Reagan

Reason and free inquiry are the only effectual agents against error.
                                                    —Thomas Jefferson

What kind of America will there be for my sons in the year 2050? Hell, I'm enjoying myself enough that I'd like to still be working away in 2050. What will that America be like?

It seemed unrealistic in 1960 to envision an African-American president. It seemed unrealistic in 1970 to envision an America in which openly gay people hold high-ranking elected office. But there were people at that time working toward those goals. Those people were true leaders and heroes. We will do the same for secularism. Let us envision the Secular America of 2050, a time in which the real values of Jefferson and Madison have come to prevail and dominate the political and civic discourse of our nation.

Whatever his faults, Jefferson was a genius nearly beyond our comprehension. One of my favorite books is *Undaunted Courage* about the journey of Meriwether Lewis and William Clark. This expedition, formally known as the Corps of Discovery, was a personal initiative of President Jefferson. What a feat of derring-do! But the vision and the sheer lust for botany, for science, for geography, for anthropology, for life? That was all Jefferson.

With Jefferson's Enlightenment vision and Madison's remarkable Constitution, we see a nation intentionally designed to evolve as it moves into the future, not to be locked in some inflexible past. This Tea Party nonsense of pretending that Americans today are supposed to behave as Americans did in 1787 is the exact opposite of what Madison intended. What might our secular future look like?

Ten Guiding Principles of a Secular America

Our rejuvenated secular America will be guided by these moral imperatives:

1. Our military shall serve and include all Americans, religious and nonreligious, with no hint of bias, and with no hint of fundamentalist extremism coloring our military decisions at home or abroad.

2. Any federal- or state-funded program, whether offering services domestic or foreign, that relates to reproductive health and intimate sexual decisions shall be based on science and public health, not on religious bias or the denigration of women or sexual minorities.

3. Health-care professionals shall fulfill their ethical and professional oath to address the needs of their patients, and they must do so with no hint of religious bias and in respectful service to the needs of the patients they are sworn to serve—or they must find another job.

4. There shall be no bias based on religion or lack thereof in any land-use planning or environmental laws, and discrimination based on religion or lack thereof shall be prohibited in any employment setting.

5. While marriage can be defined by a religion as that religion so chooses for the purposes of its internal ceremonies, our government shall never impose a religious bias on the definition of marriage.

6. When facing the end of life, all Americans shall be guaranteed control over their own bodies, without being thwarted by religious bias.

7. America's youth shall never be subjected to religious bias in education. If there is one penny of government funds involved, there must not be one iota of religious bias or propaganda.

8. The composition of our Congress and legislatures shall include Secular Americans, and there must be no political bias against secular candidates.

9. There shall be one consistent standard pertaining to the health and welfare of children, no matter the religion of a child's parents, school, or child-care center. Religious extremists can do whatever they want to their own bodies, but children shall be treated as human beings, not as pawns to be sacrificed in the name of religion.

10. Medical, technical, and scientific innovation shall be dedicated to the health and advancement of our fellow citizens and must never be impeded by religious bias.

Let us linger on this last point, for it captures something essential and inspiring. Important ideals—and real lives—are at stake. When we betray stem cell research, we betray our fellow human beings. When we betray the scientific method, we betray the human spirit at its very best.

Our cause, the cause of Secular Americans—as the principles described herein demonstrate—is sacred. That's right. Sacred. Progress today, progress in 2050, and progress a thousand years from now will be based most significantly on our commitment to Enlightenment values. Evidence will guide our conclusions. Compassion will guide our actions. This is the essence of secular social action.

This incremental improvement—step by step, piece by piece, evidence upon evidence, idea upon idea—stands as the most important guiding tool of our species. There is indeed "a grandeur to this view of life," as Darwin put it.

Our Secular Decade plan sets out achievable goals to significantly improve our nation. It will require all of us to work together with every ounce of our reason, our devotion, our passion. If together we achieve the steps I've described in this plan by 2020, we will have reached a tipping point that will lead us to an even greater America—one based on our founding principles.

Reason and Innovation from the Top of the World

America must speak from the mountaintop once again. Our great secular future—like our great secular past—will be one of innovation, of science, and of the ever-churning competition of new ideas. Our future America must be an America where the tinkerer and the garage inventor are hailed as heroes, and the shysters and "prosperity" preachers are prosecuted for misuse of funds.

JFK liked to quote Aristotle, that happiness is life lived along lines of excellence. We loved Kennedy's patriotic vision of American exceptionalism. America the beautiful? Sure. But Kennedy inspired us to be America the best. When we set the goal of sending a man to the moon, when we led in science, when we aspired to equal opportunity for all our citizens, America was indeed exceptional in the best sense of that word. We did stand out, and the world loved us for it. Kennedy's picture was in huts in Africa, in villages in India. Think of the sheer boldness of it.

Conservative columnist George Will had his finger on a central issue when he wrote in a January 2, 2011, column: "From 1970 to 1995, federal support for research in the physical sciences, as a fraction of gross domestic product, declined 54 percent; in engineering, 51 percent. On a per-student basis, state support of public universities has declined for more than two decades and was at the lowest level in a quarter-century before the current economic unpleasantness. Annual federal spending on mathematics, the physical sciences and engineering now equals only the increase in health-care costs every nine weeks."

Sadly America must look elsewhere for a glimpse of the secular America of 2050 to which we must aspire. Consider innovation in Sweden. The public and the private sectors in Sweden allocate nearly 4 percent of GDP to research and development (R&D) annually, which makes Sweden one of the countries that invest most in R&D as a percentage of GDP. Sweden tops Europe in comparative statistics both in terms of research investments as a percentage of GDP as well as in the number of published scientific works per capita.

Sweden can't be bothered with endless discussion about creationism, or about ancient sexual restrictions on women and minorities. Sweden innovates while America rehashes debates long settled elsewhere. Sweden often leads the world in medical science and is also among the top in natural science and engineering in terms of the number of scientific publications per capita.

Swedish inventors held a total of 33,523 patents in the United States as of 2007, according to the United States Patent and Trademark Office. Only ten other countries hold more patents than Sweden. Think about the size of the Swedish population to understand the scale of this accomplishment. With less than 10 million citizens, its more than thirty times smaller than the United States. Of the nine nations with more patents, eight are large-population countries. Only very secular Switzerland is a smaller country on the list, a nation (remember patent clerk Einstein) that was already a patent capital in the early twentieth century. Indeed, the industrial countries in the top ten are among the most secular nations on Earth.

How does saving a life every six minutes strike you as an accomplishment? It resulted from Volvo's capitalism and innovation with the three-point seat belt. In the book *Sweden: Up North, Down to Earth*, the authors state that "Swedes are some of the world's fastest people at adapting to new trends and ideas, and are constantly on the cusp of a groundbreaking innovation."

Sweden went from a frozen and poverty-stricken outpost in the late 1800s to the nation of the zipper and ball bearing in the twentieth century to Skype today. Swedes don't just come up with new ideas, they bring innovative ideas to market. In May 2010 Sweden ranked as the most competitive

European Union country according to the World Economic Forum, followed by two other very secular nations, Denmark and Finland.

Sweden's government also consistently ranks as one of the most transparent and noncorrupt. Phil Zuckerman writes persuasively about the quality of life in secular nations in a piece published January 16, 2011, by the Council for Secular Humanism titled "Is Faith Good for Us?"

The 2004 United Nations' Human Development Report, which ranks 177 countries on a Human Development Index, measured such indicators of societal health as life expectancy, adult literacy, per capita income, and educational attainment. According to this report, the five top nations in terms of human development were Norway, Sweden, Australia, Canada, and the Netherlands. All had notably high degrees of organic atheism. Furthermore, of the top twenty-five nations, all but Ireland and the United States were nations with some of the highest percentages of nontheism on Earth. Conversely, the bottom fifty countries of the Human Development Index lacked statistically significant levels of organic atheism.

As Zuckerman further points out, the most nontheistic nations have the lowest infant-mortality rates. The most religious nations have the highest infant-mortality rates. He reveals the same trend with regard to homicide rates. He points to a 2003 study which found that nations with the highest illiteracy rates were all highly religious. The highly irreligious nations in Scandinavia, which offer widespread sex education and birth-control access, have the lowest HIV and AIDS rates. According to a 2004 study, the most irreligious nations were the most likely to treat women and girls equally. The nations with the most sexist policies tend to be the most religious.

I will not attempt to prove here a direct causal relationship between secularism and a healthy strong society, but I will say secularism sure doesn't seem to hurt. In particular, as a strong proponent of innovation and capitalism, I am very impressed by the emphasis on R&D in Sweden, as well as on securing patents. Our nation has lost sight of innovation and quality of life as the standards for rational government decision making.

Another example: American Nobel Prize–winning economist James Heckman makes a strong, evidence-based case for early childhood education leading to economic strength. Pay for executives at America's largest firms has quadrupled—in real dollars—since the 1970s, which might be fine—if American executives made smart long-term choices. However, gearing decisions to the next quarterly report and the next golden parachute for themselves does nothing to match the more strategic decisions Swedes have made to invest in early childhood education so as to secure the excellent return on investment to which economic evidence points.

Sweden's sister country, Denmark, is rated the "most happy nation on earth" by the World Values Survey, conducted by Ron Inglehart and funded by the National Science Foundation. Average Danish citizens themselves report these highest levels of happiness. Inglehart discerns four common factors in the happiest nations: prosperity; a functioning democracy; high levels of social tolerance; and personal freedom (e.g., gender equality).

Danes are often rated, even more so than Swedes, as the most secular people on earth. Consider that high levels of social tolerance and personal freedom are very difficult to achieve in countries where religious dogma holds sway. A central tenet of fundamentalist Christianity and fundamentalist Islam is suppression of sexual minorities and opposition to many forms of equal rights for women.

As Phil Zuckerman has said, Danes and Swedes, spectacularly secular, find meaning in life through work, family, causes, traditions, nature, love, and good works. Instead of arguing about how some ancient document requires the shunning of other human beings, they address issues rationally. As a result, they have bus systems that work, pragmatic health coverage, and low crime rates. These innovative capitalist countries have the lowest church attendance of any place in the Western world. And what else do we find there? These innovative capitalist countries, according to the testimony of the people themselves, create a far better quality of life than Americans themselves report.

Saab and Volvo are respected innovators. America has a dual culture in business. The big corporate bureaucracy (think of our auto industry leading up to the 2008 disaster) and the innovators in our computer industry. Redmond, Washington, and Silicon Valley count among the most secular places in America, places of real innovation and capitalism. I love this country. My competitive blood flows, not out of hostility, but out of admiration for the Scandinavians. America must not be satisfied with its pockets of innovation—innovation must be our defining business practice.

A Culture of Innovation Protected by Jefferson's Wall

The Tea Party folks are exactly right about the Founders, but not in the way they think. The Constitution and the Enlightenment ideals of Jefferson and Madison make America, yes, exceptional, and the greatest nation in the history of the world. An eagerness to innovate must be our definitive characteristic, not some rigid adherence to the past. The Swedes of the twenty-first century can make a better case that they embody the innovative, freedom-loving values of our Founders. Religious fundamentalists are doing all they can to move America away from the values of

Madison and Jefferson. Many Tea Party folks love to play dress-up in Jefferson-era clothes, all while undermining the very ideals he espoused.

We have an opportunity to challenge ourselves and make America even better. We will get to that secular America in 2050, perhaps earlier. We have good examples of great secular results with the experience of Sweden and Denmark—and with the experience of our own past. It is up to us. This decade right now is pivotal. I pledge to devote myself to the Secular Decade plan. We must do this together. Let's make this decade count.

We must protect the religious liberties guaranteed in the Constitution, including the rights of the so-called Moral Majority and their allies to express their ideas with absolute freedom. However, special privileges based on their religious bias, or anyone's religious bias, must be removed from our laws.

We must devote ourselves to rebuilding Jefferson's wall of separation between church and state, a wall that has crumbled so terribly these last thirty years. We must reinvigorate a culture of innovation. And if we do these things, a great America will become even greater, a proud America will become even prouder. We can still catch up to and surpass our friends the Swedes and the Danes and every nation. This will happen when America chooses to. That is the American way. As Secular Americans we will join with our many good-hearted religious friends to achieve this goal—but we Secular Americans, because of the unique perspective we share with Jefferson, will lead the way.

A Future Worthy of Our History

I am very optimistic. Our vision, the secular vision, is one which increasingly finds fertile ground throughout the entire world. President Jimmy Carter has visited over 125 nations since leaving the White House. Carter said, "You hear John Lennon's song 'Imagine' used almost equally with national anthems." When the silver ball drops New Year's Eve, they play "Imagine." In numerous surveys, average citizens name "Imagine" as the greatest song of all time. Average people worldwide know the words.

Madison and Lennon had little in common. Madison was deeply educated and refined. Lennon began as an uneducated rock obsessive. Yet through their lives, Madison, a lawyer, and Lennon, a poet, each grew to care most deeply about improving the ways in which human beings treat each other and longed for a world in which we, as the Greeks wrote, tame the savageness of man and make gentle the life of the world.

Madison imagined a Constitution as a human, and humanist, mechanism, a tool evolving toward a more compassionate world, the specifics of which Madison knew he could not foresee. "Imagine," now a world anthem, constitutes a vision for the future, a longing that grows with each passing generation. The song embodies an optimism and wisdom that Lennon foresaw for his sons and future generations. Madison and Lennon call us to a humanist ideal, to a world where ancient hostilities and ancient restrictions fall away in favor of a world lit by rationality and compassion. Together we must move closer to the world Lennon and Madison so wisely imagined—but our efforts are not yet worthy of their greatness.

Secular Americans have been known for opposing a crèche in the town square. Now we must be known for organizing to stop fundamentalists from denying condoms and basic science-based education to poverty stricken people in Uganda and other parts of the developing world.

Secular Americans have been known for opposing so-called ceremonial deism such as the National Day of Prayer. Now we must be known for standing up to the theocratic legal concept that religious schools, because they are religious schools, have the right to punish children physically.

Secular Americans have been known for opposing "under God" in the Pledge of Allegiance. Now we must be known for working to oppose the big con job pulled by megaministers who live in palaces—subsidized by special tax loopholes that only they get—and stopping this vast fleecing of the American taxpayer.

Secular Americans have been known for opposing crosses on public land. Now we must be known for actively opposing textbooks that tell lies to children with our tax dollars.

Secular Americans have been known for opposing "In God We Trust" on coins. Let us now be known for stepping up to protect children from the "faith healers" who praise their own religiosity as they leave children to suffer and sometimes die.

I began this book with the story of Abraham. We should remember that story; it is part of the world's cultural heritage. But we must also remember the true story of two-year-old Amiyah White dying alone in a van. We should remember the story of fifteen-year-old Jessica Crank and her horribly torturous untreated tumor, which lead to her needless death. We cannot sit silently as Abraham is authorized to kill his child. Not in this century. Not with our laws. Not under our Constitution.

Maybe if we consider relinquishing the view that we are going to get out of this world alive and face the humble reality that what we do for others here is what lasts, then we might better remember victims like Amiyah White. Perhaps the essence of life is not policing other people's sex lives, not asking some supernatural being for favors. Perhaps the essence of life is actually doing the right thing for our fellow human beings—right here and right now.

Unless we act, more children will die, more children will suffer. Their deaths require a human and humanist call to justice, a moral imperative that connects directly to Madison's humanist Constitution. The vicious McCarthy era forced upon us "one nation under God" when we are really one nation under the Constitution. We have a moral obligation to fulfill our humanist heritage, a heritage that America's Constitution embodied first and most boldly. We Irish have a saying: we lost all the wars, but we had all the good songs. Well, the poets, the writers, the philosophers, and the greatest statesmen, they're on our side—but that's not sufficient.

Like the best goals, the Secular Decade strategic plan is both romantic and pragmatic. Together we can make our nation even greater by living our Enlightenment ideals with full passion and commitment. In this time, with this plan, we will succeed.

Afterword

Justice William Brennan was, without doubt, one of the ten most influential Supreme Court Justices in American history. I will happily debate whether he lands at number four or three on that list. But, for now, just note that conservatives, many of whom despise Brennan's legal thinking, concede that Brennan was hugely influential.

Yet, Justice Brennan's death was noted only in passing in the year-end retrospectives of 1997. You know the ones—the retrospectives we read in *Time* and *USA Today* during the news lull between Christmas and New Year's Eve. Who received the lion's share of attention? Lady Diana.

Lady Diana was beautiful, had a sensational wedding—and an even more sensational divorce—and did commendable work regarding land mines. I have no beef with her, but this juxtaposition—Lady Di's image everywhere, Justice Brennan's life rarely noted—struck me, and led me to contemplate in earnest the idea of death—and the legacy we leave behind.

In many ways, this contemplation is an extension of my own long-standing attempts at trying to come to grips with the idea of our own mortality. Even when I was younger, I thought a lot about death. The topic needn't be entirely morose. Woody Allen's movie *Love and Death* captures some essentials. *Harold and Maude* is a classic. But few can match the immortal *Life of Brian*. When dealing with death who better to learn from than the best Christ stand-in ever? *Life of Brian* should be required in all philosophy and religion classes. Graham Chapman may be dead, but his Brian will live forever. Whenever my father would talk about this or that famous person, my question was always, when did he or she die? I wanted to understand what they had gotten done and how long it had taken them to get it done.

Perhaps it's genetic. My mother has made year-end death lists for decades, assembling her own lists of notable people who have died the preceding year. Can you think of a more heartwarming tradition? When she'd share her list with me, she'd seek my reaction, measure my cultural knowledge, and educate me if there was a name I didn't know. It became something of a game for us and broadened my knowledge of the world—and of how individuals have the power to shape it. Each obituary filled in a gap in my understanding of history, but through the story of a human being who took a real shot at having some lasting impact.

So, years later, when faced with the juxtaposed deaths of Di and Brennan, I decided to begin creating my own annual lists. Just a little hobby, but designed to remember those who've made real contributions to the world and mankind. It's been fun—and edifying. If notoriety—sheer fame—is the test for one's list, then Lady Di easily surpasses Brennan. But that was not the test for me.

Let me illustrate with the two Juliuses. Julius Axelrod died in 2004. Ever heard of him? No? Most people haven't. He received a Nobel for research leading to selective serotonin reuptake inhibitors (SSRIs). My brother, who could play a mean cello and electric bass, died a number of years ago while very depressed. My brother might still be alive today had the fruits of Axelrod's work become commonplace just a few years earlier. Axelrod's work has saved countless thousands of lives. Because of his research and innovation, thousands more have lived fuller and often longer lives, despite facing mental illness. Axelrod was number six on my 2004 list. I bet you've heard of Tony Randall of *The Odd Couple* and Janet Leigh and her famed *Psycho* shower scene. The press covered those deaths with much more detail than that of Julius Axelrod. Randall and Leigh were probably fine people, but I don't see their accomplishments as comparable.

Don't get me wrong. Entertainers are artists and artists can be transformational. So, sure, Marlon Brando made my 2004 list. He changed the art of acting. I'm no science snob. But, overall, actors, whom I love to watch in a darkened theater, aren't exactly altering our world in the same way as the Juliuses.

Julius Richmond died in 2008. Richmond was the key scientist in the first studies of early childhood intervention. He led the first Head Start program and, as surgeon general, advocated against smoking. He made number seven on my 2008 list. My prediction, which I hope to see fulfilled, is that investment in educating early childhood brains (ages 0 to 5) gets widely implemented. I predict it will prove one of the most innovative and brilliant investments our species can make. Because of his creative insight, Julius Richmond will be more famous a hundred years hence than he is today. For now, the names Roy Scheider and Bettie Page, both of whom died in 2008, are far more recognizable. But as decades pass, I'm betting on Julius—and Julius.

When, as a child, I asked my father about the deaths of this or that famous person, what I really was trying to do was figure out how much time people have to make a difference. To paraphrase a Buddhist saying: given that your death is certain but the time of your death uncertain, what will you do? These famous people had at least gotten something done, I reasoned, and I wanted to understand how they'd pulled it off.

I have a friend, Harry Lonsdale, who reads the regular obituaries in his local paper. You know the ones: "Jim was an avid checkers player and attended regular meetings of the Elks." Jim may have had a much better time of it than, say, Vincent van Gogh. Fair point, no doubt, especially because there were no SSRIs available for van Gogh.

And yet . . . wouldn't you rather be van Gogh, if your choices are Jim and van Gogh? The richness—the transcendence—of what van Gogh accomplished embodies the most beautiful of human experiences. Harry tells me that when he looks at typical obituaries, he notes how little people actually get done. Harry does not mean to be condescending at all, because it is impossible to sum up a life and its meaning in a few words in the back of a newspaper, but Harry is a successful businessman and Harry wants to see results. It's a valid question. What can you show for results?

We are all playing our own version of *Beat the Clock* (if we bother to get in the game at all). On the old TV show of that name, you might lose and thus endure the indignity of having whipped cream sprayed in your face. We get issued these bodies and, as our bodies and brains grow, we learn that this game of life has different stakes than a door prize or whipped cream in the face. It is often, literally, sudden death, and in this game there's no overtime. Harry quoted to me a wise man who said, "Nothing worth doing can be accomplished in a lifetime." Agreed.

If there is no God, no afterlife—indeed, if your life on this one small planet is infinitesimally short—then it makes you humble and it might inspire you to plan more carefully.

If, on the other hand, God has it covered, if you will live forever (if you'll simply accept Jesus as your personal savior), then many things seem possible. In fact, some sweet shortcuts come to mind. You can hurt others —and terribly so—and be forgiven for that sin simply by asking a supernatural being for forgiveness. With the "forgiven" card, it's so much easier to say to oneself, "I will grab this food now. I will grab this money now. I will grab and grab and grab." Concern yourself with long-term consequences later. You can always be forgiven—and then you live forever! A convenient belief system indeed. Is this the attitude of all religious people? Certainly not. But does religion, as interpreted by millions, justify such attitudes? Yes.

Contrast this with the humbleness of understanding that your time is short. There is no candy at the end. Santa will not be there for you—no bag full of presents. Damn! No Santa. Remember when you first figured that one out? Ah well, time to grow up.

This reality forces upon us some careful thinking regarding the limited time we have to use our one and only brain in this oh-so-temporary body. This fragile mortal tool commands more respect once you realize it is the grand total of your allotted equipment, and there is no soul to float away from it later. "You are hereby allotted a consciousness for eighty-odd years. Use it as you choose for that time. Good luck! Sorry about the whole death business. Nothing personal, mind you. Game on! And all that."

I had the idea for a children's museum back in Maine. It took four years to put together, but we created something of top quality. Seeing the idea of a museum through to a multistory facility was an addictively enjoyable experience. After those years of work, I had a quote in mind for the museum wall, but some thought it morose: "We're born, we live a little while, we die. A spider's life can't help being something of a mess, with all this trapping and eating flies. By helping you, perhaps I was trying to lift up my life a trifle." Set in Maine, E. B. White's *Charlotte's Web* is a beautiful contemplation of life, bringing children face to face with death. Maine Discovery Museum was a way to lift up my life a trifle. Something real, something specific. That's about as satisfying as it gets.

As Woody Allen aptly puts it, "What you see is what you get." I, for one, strongly encourage you to, as the old song goes, "Enjoy yourself." It *is* later than you think. The greatest enjoyment, however, is reserved for those who, like Julius Axelrod and Julius Richmond, can say, yes, I made sure my body and brain did something creative, something beautiful. If we are all small specks in one corner of one solar system of one galaxy, then our greatest satisfaction derives from thoughtful service to a larger future.

If you enjoy a good meal, a drink, and a song at the pub, then don't deny yourself. I can tell you as someone who went to school in Ireland, some of my best experiences have been singing in the pub with laughs and stories traded along the way. If you've had that moment or two with a man or woman whose company you enjoyed, it's no sin. The sin-mongers and gossip-mongers are so tiresome. Squeezing the best you can from every moment is admirable and fun, but "simple" pleasures alone—especially for those who know just how short and precious this one life is—are an insufficient use of our allotted time.

Darwin said, "There is grandeur in this view of life, with its several powers, having been originally breathed into a few forms or into one; and that, whilst this planet has gone cycling on according to the fixed law of gravity, from so simple a beginning endless forms most beautiful and most wonderful have been, and are being, evolved."

And yes, Mr. Darwin, sure, a finch is terrific, a gibbon fascinating no doubt, but, for me, it's Kennedy and King, Eleanor and Franklin, Neil Armstrong and Vincent van Gogh, Madame Curie and Linus Pauling. We can't all equal them, but we can emulate them.

Our lives are far shorter than many a tortoise, our bodies weaker than many a fellow creature, our feet far slower than many more, yet we are unique and, to me, more interesting than rocks, burning stars, gorillas, and cheetahs. Rocks and stars and gorillas and cheetahs are no doubt impressive and fascinating, but we humans, uniquely aware of our own mortality, can consciously make the most of our little time. That inspires me. People inspire me.

I especially love the planners, the creators, the strivers—the ones who try to rise above their own blip of time and seek to share something of value, something creative and unique, with all who follow. I'm a lawyer, not a scientist, but my love for scientists is strong, and becomes stronger with each passing year. I'm proud that my hero, the lawyer Madison, agreed.

I feel a twinge, a sadness, anticipating what I won't know. I so much want to participate in the twenty-second century and beyond. I find the morning paper fascinating! Imagine the great wide future. I'm eager to know what will be known and invented—those unimaginable iPhones and health gizmos and universe-gazing telescopes of the future. More than that, I'd like to see the next Shakespeare, or the next Beatles, those who can create that beautiful unforeseeable creative change—and to play my small part as best I can.

The essence of Einstein's philosophy, which I most love, bears repeating: "Out yonder there was this huge world . . . the contemplation of this world beckoned as a liberation. . . . Similarly motivated men of the present and of the past, as well as the insights they had achieved, were the friends who could not be lost. The road to this paradise was not as comfortable and alluring as the road to religious paradise, but it has shown itself reliable, and I have never regretted having chosen it."

Some say death is natural, therefore good. This is an admirable, but I suspect counterfeit, sentiment—whistling past the graveyard. We want to sound noble and brave, as we should. As for me, I don't like death one tiny bit and refuse to pretend that I do. Labeling death "natural"—and therefore a positive event—is rather like those who argue food is good or bad based on "naturalness" alone. Arsenic is natural. I would not willingly drink from a cup of natural arsenic, and I'll let the entirely natural cup of death pass me by until I'm forced to drink its bitterness. I'll stick with my friends on Earth as long as I can manage. I draw my inspiration from people.

I greatly admire the spiritual. Carl Sagan said, "Science is not only compatible with spirituality; it is a profound source of spirituality."

The spirituality of certain death requires acceptance that our stake in the future springs, not from an afterlife, but from whatever ideas and creativity we can muster and then pass on—through our friends, family, and work. The greatest joy is to challenge ourselves to contribute.

I don't mean "contribute" in some prissy, earnest way. Let's squeeze all the juice from life. Drink it down! Stay in the game—until age ninety and beyond. Work steady, day to day, creating positive incremental change. Incremental improvement: it's the most beautiful use of time—and, ultimately, the most fun. With that goal ever in mind, a more gentle world is possible, a more healthy world, a more caring world.

It is all our own responsibility, our own choice, because there are no chosen people. There are no saved people. That's all myth. It's all of us choosing to help each other. Right now, today. It's entirely up to us. We are all responsible to each other.

... Come, my friends,
'Tis not too late to seek a newer world.
Push off, and sitting well in order smite
The sounding furrows; for my purpose holds
To sail beyond the sunset, and the baths
Of all the western stars, until I die.
It may be that the gulfs will wash us down;
It may be we shall touch the Happy Isles.

—Lord Alfred Tennyson

Appendix: Secular Coalition for America

Thousands attended Walt Whitman's funeral. Whitman's friend Robert Ingersoll, known as the "great agnostic," delivered the funeral oration. Ingersoll may have been the most popular public speaker in an era when speeches were a form of popular entertainment. Ingersoll's speech nominating James G. Blaine for president in 1876 was a model for Franklin Roosevelt's "Happy Warrior" speech of 1928. Ingersoll's most popular topic was ethical agnosticism. People would actually pay one dollar each, a large sum at the time, to hear him speak. Huge crowds would sit enthralled for his three-hour oratorical arias, just as today we go to a movie or concert. He was perhaps the most unequivocal and public advocate for freethinking in the 1800s when no formal freethought organization existed. Such organizations began to spring up in the late 1800s.

Just as the term "freethinkers" suggests, most secular groups traditionally remained separate from other like-minded groups with similar, if distinct, missions. It wasn't until more than one hundred years after Ingersoll's famous speeches that Herb Silverman, a mathematics professor at the College of Charleston, saw the need to connect these groups through one unifying organization. Silverman's vision united these groups in what has become the Secular Coalition for America. He did so with the help of activist Bobbie Kirkhardt, the well-connected political insider Woody Kaplan, and many others. The ten groups that today form the Secular Coalition for America have an admirable heritage and are at the vanguard of the effort against today's theocratic attack on America's founding principles.

American Ethical Union
The American Ethical Union and its respective Ethical Culture Societies (congregations) have played an important and positive role in American

social change. If you believe in the mission of the ACLU and oppose child labor, then you must thank in part the American Ethical Union. Particularly through its New York branch, it has had a major impact. In 1876, Felix Adler, a rabbi, founded the Ethical Culture movement based on his philosophy that—in essence—a naturalistic view of the world embodies a very ethical view. A dynamic speaker, Adler led the creation of Ethical Culture Societies. This philosophy represents perhaps the first expressly nontheistic religion in America. A "nontheistic religion"? It's counterintuitive, but Ethical Culturists view their moral values as a high call, a religion, and they are so recognized by the IRS. This nontheist viewpoint was revolutionary for a formal congregation, though the Unitarians and Deists (e.g., Thomas Jefferson) had earlier come close to such a viewpoint in rejecting miracles, the divinity of Christ, and the virgin birth.

Followers of Ethical Culture, by contrast, came out and simply focused on the essentials in their religion—in short, ethics. This entirely reasonable proposition flourished, particularly in the early twentieth century, when Ethical Culture Societies were so deeply involved in social change, such as in the founding of the ACLU and instituting pro bono work in the legal profession. J. Robert Oppenheimer, the brilliant nuclear physicist blacklisted for his progressive politics, was raised in Ethical Culture in New York and attended the movement's prestigious Fieldston School on the Upper West Side, a place of innovative thinking that employed the Socratic method.

Albert Einstein, a reasonably bright chap, supported the American Ethical Union. Celebrating its seventy-fifth anniversary, Einstein said, "Without 'ethical culture' there is no salvation for humanity." The connection between a naturalistic worldview and an ethical worldview is a common sense one. There is no ancient document demanding rejection or subjugation of this or that category of person in Ethical Culture.

Not long ago, I spoke at an Ethical Culture Society in the Chicago area with a very active Sunday school, partly administered by a young attorney named Carolyn Welch. Her husband, Raam Jaani, is, like me, a graduate of the University of Notre Dame. Yet their young family finds the Ethical Culture Society to be a good home for reinforcing the moral values that infuse their lives. There are many good Kennedy Catholics who no longer participate in the Catholic Church because the Scalia Catholics seem to run that outfit these days. Ethical Culture, and several of the Secular Coalition for America groups for that matter, offers a welcoming home not only for

Kennedy Catholics but also for many liberal Protestants, secular Jews, and secular Muslims. The tent is big. Jennifer Scates, the new president of American Ethical Union, has an important job—sustaining the heritage of the country's longest-standing secular organization. The religion of Ethical Culture offers a moral alternative free of punitive ancient dogma.

American Humanist Association

In 1929, the first Humanist Society of New York was founded, with Albert Einstein as an original advisory board member. The Humanist Manifesto, issued in 1933, was written primarily by Raymond Bragg, a Unitarian minister. Many Unitarians proudly carried on a tradition that extended back to Founders like the Adamses. Some, like Bragg, felt that they were part of a religion that needed to face squarely its embrace of an ethical life stance and the reality—pervasive in many Unitarian congregations—that the concept of God was more window dressing than a necessary reality in their daily lives. Bragg embraced ethical nontheism as "humanism."

To embrace humanism is to embrace the concept that caring for our fellow human beings is our highest calling. The American Humanist Association for a time filed as a religion with the IRS, in part because it had celebrants who performed weddings and funerals. However, the American Humanist Association decided that the misperception that humanism was a theistic religion confused people, so it chose to form as an expressly secular 501(c)(3) corporation. This made the organization's nontheism more clear. The organization communicates strong moral values and encourages nontheistic celebrants to officiate at major life events.

American Humanist Association board president David Niose, a well-spoken attorney, seeks the recognition of "Secular Americans" as a demographic category. Secular Americans is an umbrella term for all agnostics, freethinkers, atheists, humanists, and other nonreligious people who place their fellow human beings in the real world as those to whom they owe their paramount obligation. Dave Niose's umbrella term is wisely chosen. Secular Americans represent a distinct and valuable slice of the American demographic pie. It's entirely appropriate that various religious groups (Muslims, Catholics, etc.) are identified by population in the census results, but Bill Gates and Warren Buffet embody a form of rationalism and reasonableness that's also worthy of its own distinct demographic category.

The American Humanist Association has for some years been led by its understated and savvy executive director Roy Speckhardt. His presence has been a significant reason for its strength in the twenty-first century.

American Atheists

Madalyn Murray O'Hair stormed onto the scene in the 1960s with perhaps one or two more curse words than might be strictly necessary—yet she made quite valid constitutional points about prayer in school and numerous other issues. American Atheists has maintained its edge by design. The organization sometimes describes itself as the Marine Corps of atheism. No celebrants for weddings offered here, no churchlike services. Instead, American Atheists offers a clear, forceful rejection of religious dogma. Its past president, Ed Buckner, issued these rejections with an avuncular and folksy style reminiscent of Mark Twain. Its current president, Dave Silverman, is a forceful and unequivocal voice and a strong leader who will very likely succeed in growing this organization significantly by remaining proudly on the cutting edge. Its central mission is to bring smart lawsuits and to generally articulate the clearest and boldest cases for nontheistic positions.

Society for Humanistic Judaism

As a student of public speakers, I enjoy listening to and learning from public speakers that understand the craft. Rabbi Sherwin Wine, an excellent public speaker, died in a 2007 car crash. I wish I'd had the opportunity to hear him speak. Rabbi Wine in the mid-1960s knew there were a lot of secular Jews in America. Believing they needed a spiritual home, he founded the Society for Humanistic Judaism. Humanistic Judaism, like Ethical Culture, is a religion. If you've ever attended a Reform synagogue, as I did with my ex-wife, you might think of Humanistic Judaism as the "just-come-out-and-say-it" version of Reform Judaism. I've met numerous Jews in the Reform tradition who, like many Unitarian Universalists, are essentially agnostic or atheist—even if they don't use those terms. The Society for Humanistic Judaism is proud of its Jewish traditions and heritage. Today, it is led by its Harvard-trained board president Lou Altman and executive director Bonnie Cousens. Its rabbis celebrate at weddings, funerals, and coming-of-age ceremonies, and its synagogues hold weekly services. Many Humanistic Jews, often termed secular Jews, simply don't need the trappings of believing in the inerrancy of some ancient document to believe that you should be good to your neighbor and your family or to celebrate a proud ethnic heritage.

Council for Secular Humanism

Philosopher Paul Kurtz founded the Council for Secular Humanism in the early 1980s to advocate and defend a nonreligious life stance rooted in science, naturalistic philosophy, and humanist ethics. The council debunks supernatural claims of any sort—astrology, homeopathy, space aliens, and the like. The council's name stems, in part, from a response to the many public references to "secular humanism" by the late Jerry Falwell. Falwell, of course, used the term as a pejorative, seeing it as a font of atheistic evil. The council's current president and CEO is Ron Lindsay, and its executive director, Tom Flynn, is also editor of the excellent *Free Inquiry* magazine.

Atheist Alliance America

Atheist Alliance America, one of the newer organizations on the scene, has thrown some whiz-bang conventions. It is an umbrella organization of local affiliates in the United States. It provides support to them in terms of organizational and leadership development and assists them in carrying out nontheist actions in their local communities. Its new president, Nick Lee, is focusing this organization on local community efforts, creating the ability to respond to local issues from a nontheist perspective.

Institute for Humanist Studies

This organization works as a think tank for humanism. Founded by a grant from a key secular leader named Larry Jones, the institute produces a font of ideas and promotes educational programming in humanism. Part of its brainpower derives from Anthony Pinn, the institute's research director. Dr. Pinn, the Agnes Cullen Arnold Professor of Humanities and professor of religious studies at Rice University, earned his PhD in the study of religion at Harvard University. His work has focused on liberation theology, black religion, and black humanism. The board president is an experienced business leader, Warren Wolf.

Military Association of Atheists and Freethinkers

Jason Torpy, a West Point graduate, speaks out for thousands of members of the Armed Services who are sometimes treated as second-class citizens by the fundamentalists who make concerted efforts to impose their religion on our military and who undermine our Constitution in doing so. The change in character of the military from a religiously unaffiliated organization above politics to an organization that sometimes permits proselytizing and religious discrimination makes for a historic and regrettable story. Jason has an important job helping to return our Armed Services to their true heritage.

Secular Student Alliance

Campus Crusade for Christ has flourished for decades. This past decade, its founder provided biblical justifications for the invasion of Iraq—ideas that President George W. Bush embraced. Founded in 2000, the Secular Student Alliance offers a reasonable and rational alternative to organizations like Campus Crusade for Christ. Many young people on college campuses and in high schools wish to network with other young people who stand for what college and education are all about: free inquiry, evidence-based analysis, critical thinking, and plain old-fashioned rationalism. August Brunsman serves as executive director of the Secular Student Alliance. It turns out there are quite a few young people who believe in the collegiate ethic of closely reasoned analysis. Thus, the alliance is growing rapidly, with new chapters continuously being founded on campuses across the country and now in high schools as well.

Camp Quest

Children should be allowed to view the world freely without being boxed in. Children should not be indoctrinated as Communists or Libertarians, or Republicans or Democrats. Let them gather information and draw their own conclusions as they mature. Similarly, why is someone who is five a Catholic? The answer, of course, is she is not. A child is merely labeled by someone else when she is not old enough to consent. Why is a ten-year-old being sent to a fundamentalist school that teaches female subordination and the rejection of evolution? Amanda Metskas serves as executive director at Camp Quest, where children aren't subjected to propaganda but are instead provided with information and challenged with questions. Camp Quest offers weeklong secular summer camp programs for children ages eight to seventeen, with ten locations in America and three overseas. No one at Camp Quest forces children to embrace nontheism or any other worldview. However, children are taught to seek truth and to use critical reasoning and the scientific method to arrive at their own conclusions.

Camp Quest, founded in 2006, embodies in many ways the highest and most long-standing aspirations of the Secular Coalition for America: Will our young people have the opportunity to move to the uplands of Enlightenment reasoning? Or will they be muffled and subordinated by unjust laws, laws overtaken by religious bias embedded in ancient texts on parchment and lambskin?

Acknowledgments

Just twenty-one copies of the gorgeous Gutenberg Bible now exist. About two hundred original editions of the justly revered King James Bible still exist. The book market has changed slightly since those days. An estimated eight hundred books were published every day in the United States—before the Kindle revolution.

Among these books, there is a vast literature on the separation of church and state in particular and secularism in general—a literature chock-full of great writers. Is there something unique that I can offer? I like to entertain the thought (in the shower, when no one is listening to me sing) that I offer in this volume a distinct case for why the separation of church and state remains a pivotal and neglected issue at our time in history. In the nation that originated the concept of separation of church and state, we see how that wall has dramatically crumbled in less than four decades. I also offer what I hope is a distinct strategy for reframing the issues in a way that can garner widespread support for Mr. Jefferson's wall and a specific plan for restoration of that wall.

I'm sure this book has many flaws for which I take responsibility, but many flaws were avoided because of the wisdom of others.

Kurt Volkan, my publisher, made this book congeal by suggesting essential reorganization. His excellent paring, editing, and prodding were indispensible, and his ideas for strategically reframing elements of the book vastly improved it.

My non-Samoan attorney, Mike Schacht, went far beyond the call of "intellectual property" duty and read an early and, shall we generously say, imperfect version of this book. He improved it significantly in its first of several revisions. I appreciate that he allowed me to abuse our friendship with this imposition.

Robert Frank's newspaper-editing skills were indispensible to improving yet another draft of this book. Since childhood, I've known that Robert can cut through the blather, and I found his comments very helpful.

Serah Blain reviewed my manuscript using a blade with a serrated edge. For that I shall always be thankful. She never hesitates to be intelligently and honestly forceful, causing me to think again and revise again.

Mike Meno, Secular Coalition for America's communications manager, read an early version of a chapter of my manuscript and spoke scathingly of it. This led to helpful and needed changes.

After seeing some of my speeches early on, Robin Cornwell, of the Richard Dawkins Foundation for Reason and Science, became an advocate on my behalf, making the case that my speeches would work as the kernel of a useful book.

Todd Stiefel, of the Stiefel Freethought Foundation, drew on his successful business background to suggest improvements to the Secular Decade plan presented in chapter 9. Todd offers positive reinforcement as well as specific questions that gently highlight gaps that must be addressed. Todd and I got involved in Secular Coalition for America at almost the exact same time. In his optimism and can-do spirit, I find a mirror for what I aspire to be.

Janet Strauss and her partner Jeff Hawkins have been hugely influential in calling on me to "think big" about Secular Coalition for America. Their business sense tells them that we must all make a major investment in time, money, and human capital in order to succeed. Their vision has been essential to the success we have had so far, but perhaps even more importantly, they have made clear to me that, unless we set our sights high, we will surely fail. This book offers a pragmatic way to aim high.

Herb Silverman, president of the board of Secular Coalition for America, is one of the best writers and public speakers in secularism. His suggestions regarding a later version of this volume were wisely chosen and very helpful.

Woody Kaplan (relentless in his drive and disarming with his wit), Roy Speckhardt (steady, calm, and savvy), and Maggie Ardiente (effervescent and the embodiment of positive secularism) have been indispensible guides to my rather recent education in the secular movement. Their detailed knowledge and kindness offered to a newcomer has helped me learn the "who's who" and "what's what" necessary to making this book relevant.

Greg Stikeleather has consistently offered strategic advice pertaining to the Secular Decade plan that has aided my thinking and raised our sights. The same holds true for Michael Lewis and Amy Boyle who offered very valuable advice. Similarly, Heather Ammermuller and Bentley Davis offered valuable comments on the text.

Thank you, Richard Dawkins. He honored me by believing that my ideas could lead to a strong book that serves the vision of Jefferson and Madison. Without him, I would likely not have written this book. Rarely has an Irish-American pol been so thankful to an English gentleman.

Thank you to the many gifted writers and thinkers whose work informs and inspires me. In the selected bibliography, I note several of the books that were most helpful to me in crafting the arguments offered in these pages, and I am especially grateful to their authors.

Thank you to the entire staff at Secular Coalition for America. We together must face the nuts and bolts necessary to reach our goals. It is bold and exciting work, and I am proud to work with them.

I owe my mother, Jan Spicer, unique editing kudos. In years past, I wrote regular columns for my hometown daily paper and for a monthly magazine. With these columns, as with my speeches, I always looked to my mother for the ability to turn a 1,000-word piece into a 700-word piece, all while retaining the essence of the material. My mother applied those same skills to this manuscript many times. With the exception of Kurt Volkan, no one read this manuscript so thoroughly and I am forever thankful.

I thank Aymie Walshe. Ever since I wrote an editorial for my high-school paper (supporting equal treatment for gay teachers), I've been fascinated by the goal of persuading people to causes in which I passionately believe. Logic is essential but insufficient. The arrangement of words, leading to a crescendo, lies at the heart of persuasive speaking and writing. Aymie possesses a theatrical instinct for how a written text will translate into emotion and action. The title of this book was her idea.

Finally, I thank my good-hearted sons. I ask that they always remember these profound and immortal words from *Life of Brian*:

Brian: "You are all individuals."
The crowd in unison: "Yes, we're all individuals!"
A lone voice: "I'm not."

Selected Bibliography

Many books that deal with the separation of church and state and America's secular heritage informed this book, but those that most directly influenced this book and to which I am most indebted include:

Allen, Brooke. *Moral Minority: Our Skeptical Founding Fathers*. Chicago: Ivan R. Dee, 2006.

Boston, Robert. *Why the Religious Right Is Wrong about Separation of Church and State*. Amherst, NY: Prometheus Books, 1993.

Dwyer, James G. *Religious Schools v. Children's Rights*. Ithaca and London: Cornell University Press, 1998.

Ehrenreich, Barbara. *Bright-Sided: How Positive Thinking Is Undermining America*. New York: Metropolitan Books, 2009.

Hamilton, Marci A. *God vs. Gavel: Religion and the Rule of Law*. New York: Cambridge University Press, 2005.

Jacoby, Susan. *Freethinkers: A History of American Secularism*. New York: Metropolitan Books, 2004.

Ketchum, Ralph. *James Madison: A Biography*. Charlottesville, VA: University of Virginia Press, 1990.

Kramnick, Isaac, and R. Laurence Moore. *The Godless Constitution: The Case against Political Correctness*. New York: W. W. Norton & Company, 1997.

Peters, Shawn Francis. *Prayer Fails: Faith Healing, Children, and the Law*. New York: Oxford University Press, 2007.

Putnam, Robert, and David E. Campbell. *American Grace: How Religion Divides and Unites Us*. New York: Simon & Schuster, 2010.

Sharlet, Jeff. *The Family: The Secret Fundamentalism at the Heart of American Power*. New York: Harper Collins, 2008.

Index

About the Author

Sean Faircloth served five terms in the Maine Legislature on both the judiciary and appropriations committees. In his last term, he was elected Majority Whip by his caucus colleagues.

Faircloth had the idea for the Maine Discovery Museum and led the four-year project from conception to completion in 2001. Of the twenty-five children's museums in New England, the Maine Discovery Museum was then the second-largest children's museum outside Boston.

An accomplished legislator, Faircloth successfully spearheaded over thirty laws, including the so-called deadbeat-dad child-support law that saved Maine taxpayers hundreds of millions of dollars and became a model for federal law. Faircloth had numerous legislative successes in children's issues and justice-system reform.

Faircloth has spoken around the United States about the Constitution, children's policy, obesity policy, and sex-crime law. He chaired a commission on sex-crime-law reform that led to substantive improvement in that area of law. He also chaired a commission on early childhood, as well as a commission regarding the citizen-initiative process.

Faircloth graduated from the University of Notre Dame and has a law degree from the University of California Hastings College of the Law. He served as a state assistant attorney general and as a lobbyist for the Maine State Bar Association.

In 2009 Faircloth became executive director of the Secular Coalition for America, advocating for separation of church and state and for greater acceptance of nontheist viewpoints in American life. As executive director of Secular Coalition for America, he conceived of and drafted the Secular Decade plan, and has worked with the Coalition's board and staff and many others to continually improve this plan, which offers a specific strategy for returning America to its secular roots.